I KNOW YOU PRAY,
BUT
WHAT IS PRAYER?

For Irene, my confidant and greatest encourager.

Printed in the United States of America
Keen Vision Publishing, LLC
www.publishwithkvp.com
ISBN: 978-1-955316-73-6

I KNOW YOU PRAY, BUT WHAT IS PRAYER?

A BOOK ON UNDERSTANDING PRAYER
Patrick H. Tisdale, Jr.

TABLE OF CONTENTS

THE ALTAR OF SEVEN BIBLES

Rehoboth Baptist Church was founded and established by God; it was all of Him based on what is written in Genesis 26:18-25 of the quarreling over wells being dug. Isaac, the servant of God, moved on, and finally, a well was dug over which there was no arguing, and he named it Rehoboth. The appearance of the Lord to Abraham was a soul-wrenching experience, and he built an altar there and called upon the name of the Lord. A similar experience was afforded me the night of the first business meeting of the newly-formed church. The Lord revealed to me that He wanted the church to be a *theocracy* and not a *democracy,* and upon receiving God's directives as to how the church would be governed, it was sealed by The Altar of Seven Bibles.

Upon the directive being received and the people saying *"all that the Lord has said we will do,"* instructions were given of the Lord to ask seven people to bring up their Bibles, and then they were stacked on top of each other. The people knelt before them on a cold concrete floor, and prayer was offered up to God to commit that the church would be governed as a *theocracy*.

When the people rose from their knees and returned to their seats with their Bibles, then the Lord spoke to me to erect The Altar of Seven Bibles to sit beside the pulpit. I told the people what the Lord had told me to do. One member had purchased two Bibles that day, and she brought them up, and another member gave forty dollars to purchase the other five. Later, instruction was given by the Lord to encase them and give the casing the appearance of being covered in gold.

The picture on the front cover is an actual altar that sits beside the pulpit in Rehoboth Baptist Church, the place of worship the Lord provided us. Then, on June 5, 1996, the altar led the way in a five-mile march that began in a rainstorm, but about a quarter of a mile from the church, the rain ceased, and the sun appeared. The Altar of Seven Bibles led us into the sanctuary and was placed in its permanent position by the pulpit. I offered prayer as Solomon offered a prayer to God in the temple's dedication that anyone who came in before The Altar and prayed, God would hear from heaven and answer them.

PREFACE

Why another book on prayer? Some are likely to conclude that the present work is but another addition to the already overwhelming number of studies on the subject of prayer. There are nearly as many methods of praying as there are nationalities of people in the world. Thus I wondered whether a new book should be added to an already confused picture.

I Know You Pray But What Is Prayer? is a study that grew from personal experiences. On June 5, 1986, I walked off a lucrative job to be a full-time pastor at the Oak Hill Baptist Church in Bolivar, Tennessee. I worked in quality control at a factory then known as Dover Corporation, an elevator company based out of Horn Lake, Mississippi, with a factory in Middleton, Tennessee. My job at that time consisted of being able to move all over the plant, inspecting various jobs for accuracy in their assembly before being shipped. I found myself spending a lot of time with God in meditation, and while in the heat of the meditation, I was paged to come and inspect a job. I had to turn God loose and focus on my job. I got tired of the interruptions, and through much prayer and meditation with God, I was led to go full-time in the ministry. I made it a practice upon going full-time to always be at the church on Sunday morning between 5:00 and 5:30 AM, to spend time along with the Lord, and 40 years later it is still an enjoyable practice. It is a great delight to be there with the Lord before the congregation arrives.

Being full-time positioned me to spend quality time with God in prayer. Then upon His establishing Rehoboth Baptist Church in Jackson, Tennessee, the Lord took me to Himself and commanded me to lead the church He was establishing. This church I have served since March 4, 1995, to the present. No teaching material was purchased during the first seven years of the church's existence. Instead, I prepared everything the congregation was taught. As a result, I prepared over three hundred Biblical topics to fit the congregation's needs, one of which is the material compiled.

Here is a book that fills a great need in Christian literature, covering as it does the main branches of truth relating to the Christian in prayer. Careful distinctions are made between truths often puzzle Christians in their study of this great theme, such as the differences between prayer and meditation. In addition, the questions most asked concerning the believer's present life when it comes to prayer are: *What are the advantages of prayer? Does prayer work? Am I praying right? What is the right way to pray?* These are some of the topics very thoroughly examined and answered. This present book is written for the busy pastor and the interested layman. There are terms of a nontechnical nature to express observations derived from technical study. Many sermons and devotional ideas will be found in this book, but most of all, the reader will understand the meaning of prayer and what prayer is. He or she will be inspired by what is involved in effective praying.

More than a read for the ordained minister, this is a book about the lifestyle of every Christian. This is a personal book written from my own experience, and it will speak to others seeking to have the spirit of prayer transform their lives as it has mine.

INTRODUCTION

There is a serious misunderstanding when it comes to prayer. I had a spiritual awakening that prayer was much more than what I had been led to believe. I received a challenge around the middle of the year of our Lord 1999 from a member of the Rehoboth Baptist Church. Her name was Djuana Jackson Tomlin, and she was wrestling with how to pray effectively at the time. She approached me as her pastor and asked, "Will you teach us about prayer?"

I somewhat ignored her and said within my spirit, "Everybody knows how to pray. All she needs to do is get on her knees at night before she goes to bed and pray." That was my understanding because that was the way I was brought up. As a child, my parents taught me to say my prayers before I went to bed. I would pray:

Lord, lay me down to sleep.
I pray the Lord my soul to keep.

If I should die before I wake,
I pray the Lord my soul to take.
Now, bless mama, and bless daddy.
Amen.

Mrs. Tomlin had been bowing on her knees in prayer, but she was still unfulfilled, so she kept troubling me with the question, "When will you teach us how to pray?" She persisted for some four to five months. Upon her persistence to be taught about prayer, a study of teaching on prayer began in December 1999 entitled "What is Prayer?" and the preaching on prayer began in January 2000 with a seven-part series of sermons on prayer entitled "Barriers to Answered Prayer," scripture text Zechariah 7:11-13. I include the first sermon as a part of this introduction, as it was preached on the first Sunday in January 2000. Five of the sermons on "Barriers to Answered Prayer" were revised and preached again in 2016. They are also included in this book.

Barriers to Answered Prayer - Part One
Sermon Delivered January 2000

The Lord is directing me to deal with what will bar our prayers from being heard, that which is a stumbling block, an obstacle, a hindrance, a deterrent, a hurdle that our prayers have to clear. There are barriers to answered prayer. Israel was a people of God's choice, a nation He used to reveal Himself to other nations. Paul recognizes this in his writing to the Romans. He says, "*For whatsoever things were written beforehand were written for our learning that we through patience and comfort of the scripture might have hope.*" (Romans 15:4). Israel had the wrong understanding of God. They did a lot of assuming with God, and it's pretty much the same today regarding God and what we want. We go on assumptions rather than facts. Israel had an inadequate view of things that became strong barriers to their prayers being answered.

They had an inadequate view of prayer and God's will. When you look at prayer as it relates to the Word of God, we find an interesting statement about the link between prayer and the Word of God. It says, "*Your ancestors would not listen to my messages. They turned stubbornly away and put their fingers in their ears to keep from hearing. They made their hearts as hard as stone, so they could not hear the law or the messages that the Lord Almighty had sent them by his Spirit through the earlier prophets. That made the Lord Almighty very angry with them, and since they refused to listen when He called to them, He would not listen when they called to Him, says the Lord Almighty.*" (Zechariah 7:11-13) Zechariah explained to the people what brought the great wrath of God down on them by hardening their hearts. Any sin seems more natural to do the second time. Therefore, as we become hardened, each repetition is easier. Ignoring or refusing God's warning will harden you each time you do wrong. Read God's Word and apply it to your life. Sensitivity and submission to God's Word can soften your heart and allow you to live as you should. The purpose of prayer, reading God's Word, and coming to teaching is to discover God's Will. Now in order for prayer to be effective, it must go hand in hand with the Word of God. The Word says, "*If we ask anything according to his will, he hears us.*" (1 John 5:14).

The will of God is in the Word of God. The emphasis here is on God's will, not our will. When we communicate with God, we don't demand what we want; rather, we discuss with Him what He wants for us. When we align our prayers to His will, He will listen; and we can be certain that He will give us a definite answer if He listens. Remove the barrier and start praying with confidence! Israel had rejected God's Word and disobeyed His commands. Therefore the Lord would not respond to their prayers. Zechariah says they made their hearts as adamant stone (very hard) lest they should hear the law and the words he had sent in his Spirit by the prophet. Therefore came great anger from the Lord of Hosts. It came to pass that as God cried through prophets, they would not hear, so when they cried to God, He would not hear them.

In this passage of scripture, God is saying that because you will not hear the man of God when he preaches or proclaims my Words to you, I will not hear you when you cry unto me in prayer. These verses have grave implications for us today. God treats us the way we treat His Word. It is paramount that we realize what this is saying. How we listen to sermons is important. The Word says, "*Therefore we ought to give the more earnest heed to the things we have heard lest at any time we let them slip or we drift away.*" (Hebrews 2:1) You see, familiarity breeds contempt, that is having a lack of respect or reverence for something. When we become hard and callous, refusing to listen to preaching, it concerns God greatly. Don't try to make a prerogative of God meaningless. He says, "*...How can they hear without a preacher, and how can they preach except they be sent?*" (Romans 10:14-15). Therefore we must listen to sermons and obey God's Word. Then the Lord will not turn a deaf ear to our prayers for help. I hear you saying that this can't be because He is merciful, and we are under grace. That is true, but do you understand what mercy is? It keeps God from giving you what you deserve. So when He lets you keep living, just barely making it, you are getting mercy from Him. And grace is the unmerited favor of God, whereas He just lets you float along, but you could have it so much better if you only obeyed Him.

Not only did the Israelites have a very inadequate view of prayer. At the root of these misconceptions was their inadequate view of the will of God. The people didn't realize that God's will involves five characteristics. (1) What should be done, (2) Who should do it, (3) How it should be done, (4) Why it should be done, and (5) When it should be done. This is something that needs to be realized by the child of God. If God didn't follow through with these five characteristics of His will, it would just be a thought on God's part, and the rest is left up to us. God does not leave it up to us. Wherever God's will is concerned, He directs it all the way. God had told the Israelites that it was His will that they go into the Promised Land (What). You will be led by Joshua (Who). You will possess the land by my power (How).

For my glory (Why). God said to them, "*I don't want you to wait, but go in immediately and conquer the land relying on my guidance and power (When).*" The people didn't follow God's instructions. They ignored His will and followed their own plan. While they wanted to enter the Promised Land, they wanted to do it their way and in their time. When we do this, we miss out on what God has for us. "*Let us therefore fear lest a promise being left of us entering into His rest, any of you should seem to come short of it.*" (Hebrews 4:1). The Greek phrase *come short* means arrive too late.

Don't play around with the will of God and His Word. The Lord hates presumption, false confidence, and self-will. Israel presumed that because they had admitted their sins, God would still help them conquer the land.

There were so many within the church that were missing the teaching of prayer, and my heart grieved for them. They presumed that they knew all about prayer and how to approach God, but they were allowing themselves to be robbed by the devil. They were told in the sermon that consequences come with sin, as wetness comes with water, and scent comes with odor. It's naturally built in, and every sin has its own consequence. Many of us are experiencing the consequences of our sins, and we think God is against us and won't answer our prayers. However, He had nothing to do with what you are going through. You brought that on yourself. The sermon ended, telling them that they needed to understand God's will and how to approach Him in prayer. You just don't approach God just any kind of way, and He will hear and answer your prayer. As a resource for you, the reader, four more of the sermons entitled "Barriers to Answered Prayer" are at the end of this book in the form they were preached.

The Holy Spirit continued to inspire sermons on prayer for ten months, and the teachings on prayer continued for better than eleven months. What God revealed to me concerning prayer revolutionized my life. Now I understand prayer. To pray is the joy of my life. I live each day to pray. I know that to live physically, I have to take in a breath of air and return it. To live spiritually, I have to pray in the spirit through my thought life, communicating with God, and He communicates back with me because prayer is the Christian's vital breath.

This publication is dedicated to my wife Irene, who is my confidant and greatest encourager, as I shared with her the revelations God had given me on prayer. The information in this book on prayer revolves around the past 30 years of my life. It was June 5, 1986, when I went full-time as a pastor believing God's Word. "*Even so hath the Lord ordained that they which preach the gospel should live of the gospel.*" (1 Corinthians 9:14).

This is what God has revealed to me concerning prayer, and my life has been revolutionized. It is my sincere desire that you will experience the same.

I hope this book on understanding prayer will help change your life as much as it has changed mine over the past 16 years of labor in compiling this information on prayer. I pray that this book blesses all who read it as much as it has blessed me in my writing experience. I pray this book will help lead to a spiritual awakening that will deepen your understanding of prayer and enhance your intimate relationship with God so that your life will be transformed just as mine has been. Therefore, be blessed by *I Know You Pray, But What Is Prayer?*

WHAT IS PRAYER?

My dear readers, the topic *What is Prayer* opens with an understanding of prayer far from the common understanding. When it comes to prayer or praying, it is believed to be something done effortlessly on the part of the person who is praying. I venture to say that the only prayer that requires little effort is the prayer of an unsaved person. He or she can utter three words, and God will hear them. They simply have to say, "Lord, Have Mercy!" and without hesitation, God responds. It is not that simple once you are saved and have a relationship with the Lord. Prayer then becomes a means of developing you, returning you to the image that was marred by Adam. Prayer is a transforming agent of the Lord over against receiving something from the Lord, as most believe. I know this because of what it has done for me. My life has been transformed through praying throughout the day, and keeping company with the

Lord, for prayer is the Christian's vital breath, meaning just as one has to breathe to live physically, one has to pray to live spiritually. With the understanding I have now from a mental perspective, I'm always praying. To my understanding, the Bible was written to and for people that have a relationship with Him to guide and instruct them in the ways of God. A genuine relationship with God always leads to fellowship with God. Unlike the sinner, the believer must realize that he has a role to understand and perform in his praying to God. For him, prayer is an act of humble worship in which we seek God with all our hearts.

And ye shall seek me, and find me when ye shall search for me with all your heart.

Jeremiah 29:13

God is very affectionate toward those who seek Him.

I love them that love me, and those that seek me early shall find me.

Proverbs 8:17

Humble people focus more on God and others than themselves. The word *seek* in Hebrew means *to resort to; to go in search of; look for; to try to discover,; to ask for; or to try to acquire or gain.* Note we have to *seek* God. Many have been deceived by a saying that was handed down from generation to generation. The saying: "*You make one step toward God, He'll make two toward you.*" I was told that saying by my parents when I was a child, and I believed it. I didn't find out that they had the wrong understanding until I went full-time in the ministry. I went and purchased a strong concordance, and I searched and searched for the saying, *"you make one step toward God, and He will make two toward you,"* and I could not find it. The Lord let me agonize over that saying. Then one day, I was sitting in my office reading James 4:8, and when the Spirit of the Lord opened my understanding. He spoke to my heart (mind), saying that's where my parents got the saying from. It was a misinterpretation James 4:8 that says, *"Draw nigh to God, and He will draw nigh to you."* God doesn't come to you more than you come to Him. There is an equal amount of coming; He comes to you as you come to Him, but the first person is you. He starts coming to you once you start drawing nigh unto Him.

Solomon made a request of God to hear His people whenever they called to Him, even after they had sinned, done evil, and acted wickedly. Solomon prayed:

...if they turn to you with their whole heart (mind) and soul and pray toward the land you gave to their ancestors, toward this city you have chosen, and toward this Temple I have built to honor your name, then hear their prayers from heaven where you live. Uphold their cause and forgive your people who have sinned against you.

2 Chronicle 6:38-39

God responded to Solomon with the following words:

If my people who are called by my name will (1) HUMBLE themselves (2) PRAY (3) SEEK my face and (4) TURN from their wicked ways, then I will hear from heaven and will forgive their sins and heal their land.

2 Chronicle 7:14

God gives us four conditions to be met before He will hear and answer prayer. This is not realized by most because the idea of prayer is not approaching God from a sense of unworthiness. The instruction God gave Solomon must be followed in the order in which it was given. I found out that this requires labor, an engaging of the mind, thinking, reflecting, and rightly seeing Jesus for what He has done for us and is doing for us on a continual basis before the Father.

There is a great big four-letter word in 2 Chronicle 7:14 that many pay no attention to. It is *THEN*. God says when you meet all four requirements, *THEN I* will hear from heaven and forgive their sin and heal their land. In my experience of genuine praying, my life has flipped. There was a time God would have to break in on the things of the world that were cluttering my mind, making it easy to push God aside. Now it is just the opposite. The things of the world are trying to break in on God, and it is easy now for me to push that aside and keep meditating in prayer to God.

BIBLICAL HUMILITY

The first requirement God had of the people were to humble themselves. So what is biblical humility? It is a freedom from arrogance that grows from recognizing that all we have and are comes from God. Biblical humility is not a belittling of oneself but an exalting or praising of others, especially God and Christ.

He must increase, but I must decrease.

John 3:30

Let nothing be done through strife or vainglory, but in lowliness of mind let each esteems other better than themselves.

Philippians 2:3

Humble people focus more on God and others than on themselves. Humble yourself by your sins: Don't be overconfident, coupled with arrogance, thinking you ought to be blessed because of something you have done. We must remember Proverbs 28:13, *"He that covered his sins shall not prosper: but whoso confesses and forsakes them shall have mercy."* Seek God continually. There is a lot of evasiveness when it comes to God. We avoid God because we don't want to know ourselves. After all, when we confront God, He will show us that we are not all we think we are. Prayer is not just for us to receive from God but for God to get His hands on us. He can only mold and shape us when we are in His hands.

But now, O LORD, thou art our father; we are the clay, and thou our potter; and we all are the work of thy hand.

Isaiah 64:8

There are many other scriptures that present this same fact. Unfortunately, God has to delay answering our prayers because once they are answered, we take ourselves out of His hand and go on about our business, hindering Him from molding and shaping us into what He wants us to be. We must connect to the power source and stay connected, purposing to give our thoughts to Him throughout the day. Biblical humility is recognizing that by ourselves, we are inadequate, without dignity, and worthless. Yet, because we are created in God's image and because, as believers, we are in Christ, we have infinite worth and dignity. True humility does not produce pride but gratitude. Because God is personal, all people can offer prayers. However, sinners who have not trusted Jesus Christ for their salvation remain alienated from God. So while unbelievers may pray, they do not have the basis for a rewarding fellowship with God. They have not met the conditions laid down in the Bible for effectiveness in prayer. Christian disciples recognize that they are incapable of passing over their Creator. They have every reason to express gratitude for God's blessings, but they have far more reason to respond to God than this. They respond to the love of God for them. God's love is revealed through the incarnation and life of Christ, His atoning provision at the Cross, His resurrection, and His continuing presence through the Holy Spirit.

Devout good works in a needy world cannot replace prayer. As important as services to others are, at times, we must turn away from them and to God, who is distinct from all things and over all things. Neither should prayer be thought of as a mystical experience in which people lose their identity in the infinite reality. Effective prayer must be an informed scriptural response of persons saved by grace to the living God, who can hear and answer on the basis of Christ's payment of the penalty that sinners deserve. As such, prayer involves several important aspects. Seek God continually. Again the word *seek* means to resort to; to go in search of; look for; to try to discover; to ask; or to try to acquire or gain. Many do not feel that it is necessary to seek God, but when we seek Him, we give Him an opportunity to show us that we are not where we should be in our relationship with Him. And that within itself is very humbling. Therefore there is a lot of evasiveness on our part, a lot of avoiding God because we don't want to turn from our sinful behavior. To turn means to do an about-face and go in the opposite direction. True repentance is more than talk; it is changed behavior. Whether we sin individually, as a group, or as a nation, following these steps will lead to forgiveness. God will answer our earnest prayers. The Psalmist gives us an example:

For I am waiting for you, O Lord. You must answer for me, O Lord my God. I prayed, "Don't let my enemies gloat over me or rejoice at my downfall. I am on the verge of collapse, facing constant pain. But I confess my sins; I am deeply sorry for what I have done.

Psalms 38:15-18

PRAYER BEGINS WITH HUMILITY

But if we confess our sins to him, He is faithful and just to forgive us and to cleanse us from every wrong. If we claim we have not sinned, we are calling God a liar and showing that His word has no place in our hearts (mind).

1 John 1:9

Confession is supposed to free us to enjoy fellowship with Christ. It should ease our consciences and lighten our cares. But some Christians do not understand how it works. They feel so guilty that they confess the same sins over and over. Then they wonder if they might have forgotten something. Other Christians believe that God forgives them when they confess, but if they died with unconfessed sins, they would be forever lost. A theologian named Robert S Peterson, a spiritual counselor, told the story of a lady who kept saying she confessed her sins to God, but she didn't feel forgiven, so she kept on confessing because she didn't feel forgiven. She had to be challenged with the question, "Are you calling God a liar?"

Forgiveness is not based on your feelings but on what His Word says. When one fails to apply 1 John 1:9, they do not understand that God wants to forgive us. He allowed His beloved Son to die just so He could offer us pardon. When we come to Christ for salvation, He forgives all the sins we have committed or will ever commit. Now, this is not a license to sin, but it does say that we don't need to confess the sins of the past all over again, and we don't need to fear that God will reject us if we don't keep our slate perfectly clean.

Now we should continue to confess our sins, but not because failure to do so will make us lose our salvation. Our relationship with Christ is secure. Instead, we should confess so that we can enjoy maximum fellowship and joy with him. True confession also involves a commitment not to continue in sin. We wouldn't be genuinely confessing our sins to God if we planned to commit them again and just wanted temporary forgiveness. We should also pray for strength to defeat temptation the next time we are faced with it.

Finally, I confessed all my sins to you and stopped trying to hide them. I said to myself, 'I will confess my rebellion to the Lord.' And you forgave me! All my guilt is gone.

Psalms 32:5

What is confession? To confess our sin is to agree with God, acknowledging that He is right to declare what we have done as sinful and that we are wrong to desire or to do it. It is to affirm our intention of forsaking that sin in order to follow Him more faithfully. If God has forgiven us for our sins because of Christ's death, why must we confess our sins? In admitting our sins and receiving Christ's cleansing, we are agreeing with God that our sin truly is sin and that we are willing to turn from it. Not to turn is to rebel, and 1 Samuel 15:23 says, *"rebellion is as the sin of witchcraft and stubbornness is as iniquity and idolatry."* This will ensure that we don't conceal our sins from Him and consequently from ourselves. The emphasis is on concealing our sins from ourselves; that is what's important to God. He knows for Proverbs 15:3 says, *"the eyes of the LORD are in every place, beholding the evil and the good."* People who cover over their sins will not prosper. But if they confess and forsake them, they will receive mercy (Proverbs 28:13). Note the two things to be done before receiving mercy, we must *confess* and *forsake*. It is human nature to hide our sins or overlook our mistakes. But it is hard to learn from a mistake you don't acknowledge making. This is why we need one another. A friend on the outside looking in can see much more than the person in the game; this is what justifies coaches in sports. A good illustration is in a simple little game called Checkers that we played a lot growing up. As children, we didn't have television. We listened to a radio station called WDXI out of Nashville, Tennessee. There was a lot of static because we couldn't get the frequency clearly. I have both played checkers and watched others play. While playing, I could not see certain moves that would win me the game because I was in the game, and I would often lose. But while watching others play, standing on the outside looking on, I could see both players missing moves that would win them the game. One cannot see while they are in the game what another can see looking on. We all should pray to God for true friends. The children of God need to be able to apply the scriptures.

Confess your faults one to another, and pray one for another, that ye may be healed. The effectual fervent prayer of a righteous man availeth much.

James. 5:16

And what good is a mistake if it doesn't teach you something? To learn from an error, you need to do four things:

(1) admit it
(2) confess it
(3) analyze it
(4) make adjustments

This ensures that the error doesn't happen again. Everybody makes mistakes, but only fools repeat them. Other scriptures that need to be understood are written in the book of Hebrews. It takes humility to accept this scripture:

And you have forgotten the exhortation which speaks to you as to sons: "My son, do not despise the chastening of the Lord, nor be discouraged when you are rebuked by Him; for whom the Lord loves He chastens, and scourges every son whom He receives." If you endure chastening, God deals with you as with sons; for what son is there whom a father does not chasten? But if you are without chastening, of which all have become partakers, then you are illegitimate and not sons.

Hebrews 12:5-8

There is a tendency among Christians to view everything unpleasant that happens to them as coming from the devil. The first response you hear from people when something happens is *that old devil* or *it's nothing but the devil.* We often explain our hardship as Satan's determined attacks against us rather than admitting that we may be under the disciplinary hand of God. What is often mistaken as Satan's attack may actually be chastisement from our loving Heavenly Father. When we don't obey God, it is a sin, and there are consequences that we have to face for committing sin. Now sin upon confession is forgiven, but that has nothing to do with the consequences. The minute that we are faced with some kind of problem, we immediately, through prayer, ask God to remove it. It would be foolish to pray to God for Him to ease your discomfort when God is chastising you in order to gain your attention and bring about a necessary change in your life, but that will never happen if we keep giving credit for our troubles to the devil. Do you not know that if you are God's child, the devil can't get to you without God's permission? (Job 1:8) How tragic it is that people fail to make the connection between their problems and God's discipline.

If you are His child, He is going to correct you through chastisement, and here is where we need to appreciate it. He says that if you be without chastisement, you are not His child. Therefore I welcome the chastisement of God in my life because it means that I'm His child. Now, not all hardships are chastisement from the Lord. Some are from the bad choices that we make. If one misunderstands God's chastening them, they may actually blame God for not answering their prayers or failing to protect them from the devil when God is trying to warn them of the danger they face because of their sin. God's nature is perfect love, and He corrects us because he has our best interest at heart. No one loves us as He loves us.

ASKING FOR GUIDANCE, WAITING FOR DIRECTION

The Bible gives us an example of what will happen when we fail to ask for guidance and wait for God's direction.

And Saul built an altar to the Lord, the first one he had ever built. Then Saul said, 'Let's chase the Philistines all night and destroy every last one of them.' His men replied, 'We'll do whatever you think is best.' But the priest said, "Let's ask God first.

I Samuel 14:35-36

After being King for several years, Saul finally built his first altar to God, but only as a last resort. Throughout Saul's reign, he consistently approached God only after he had tried everything else. Like many people today, Saul assumed what God wanted instead of consulting God as to whether or not his actions were what God wanted done. This was in sharp contrast to the priest, who suggested to consult God first. How much better it would have been for Saul if he had gone to God first in building an altar as his first official act as King over against making God a last resort.

Saul was typical of people today in respect of making God a last resort. I once did as most, praying after I had tried everything I could to do, not knowing I was only making things worse. I know now that God is too great to be an afterthought. When we turn to Him first, we will never have to turn to Him as a last resort, but with far too many believers, that's what God is, an afterthought.

What happens when God is an afterthought or a last resort? We get so deep in trouble that when we finally turn to God, it is a while before we realize He has answered our prayers because of all the consequences we have to bear because we made Him an afterthought, a last resort. I know what it is to be in that predicament. I made Him a last resort when I went full-time as a pastor. I assumed on God when the church of which I was then the pastor refused to support my family and me full-time, though they were well able to do so. I maxed out about five major credit cards with a four to five-thousand-dollar credit limit. I sunk myself so deep in debt that when He did bless me financially by sending me to another church with my salary doubled and with benefits, I couldn't see the blessing because of the consequences I had to bear for not waiting on God for direction.

INTIMACY WITH GOD

The Bible gives us the strongest example that can be given about the need to have an intimate relationship with God.

The next morning, Jesus awoke long before daybreak and went out alone into the wilderness to pray.

Mark 1:35

Note that Jesus prayed early in the morning. He began His day with prayer. We had it backward. We prayed when we went to bed, perhaps because of how we were raised as children. We were taught to pray at night when we went to bed. We were trained to pray when there were no challenges to be faithful. One is not challenged while they are sleeping. The challenge to be faithful is throughout the day in the throes of the world's temptations. There is no better reason to pray in the morning than this. Christ did it, therefore He knew what was ahead for Him to face; we don't.

This, among many others, is why we should pray in the morning at the beginning of the day and then at night when we go to bed, just declare our faithfulness to Him. One writer says when you have walked with Him all day long, you don't have to bow down at night. You can just say, "Good Night, Lord," and go to bed. But from out of tradition,many of us still bow down at night. Jesus took time to pray.

Finding time to pray is not easy, but prayer is the vital link between God and us. Like Jesus, we must break away from others to talk with God, even if we have to get up early in the morning to do it! Jesus had to get up very early just to spend time alone with His Father. If Jesus needed solitude and used the early morning for prayer and refreshment, how much more is this true for us? Don't become so busy that life becomes a flurry of activity, leaving no room for quiet fellowship with God in prayer. No matter how much you have to do, you should make time to be alone with God and incorporate prayer into whatever you are doing.

O Lord, hear me as I pray; pay attention to my groaning. Listen to my cry for help, my King and my God, for I will never pray to anyone but you. Listen to my voice in the morning, O Lord, each morning I bring my requests to you and wait expectantly.

Psalms 5: 1- 3

The secret of a close relationship with God is to pray to Him earnestly each morning. In the morning, our minds are fresh before the problems of the day begin to crowd in. It is then that we can commit the whole day to God. Regular communication helps any friendship and is necessary for a strong relationship with God. Relationships are formed through frequent communication, not just talking with one another. Questions are bound to arise. I know now that there is nothing wrong with asking God questions. Questioning generates communication which forms a friendship. Satan doesn't want you and the Lord talking; therefore, he tells us to accept whatever happens and not ask God why this is happening to us. It is not a sin to question God. As a matter of fact, He wants you to ask because then you and God will be talking through your mind, which is spirit, and God is a Spirit. We need to communicate with God daily.

I learned that praying won't take away from your work, but will make it more successful. Begin your day like Jesus did in a solitary place early in the morning. Now if you work second or third shift, it's when you get up. It has also been revealed to me, and I have shared it with the church, that sometimes God will wake you up, and you can't go back to sleep. That is God's way of letting you know He wants to talk, and that within itself is prayer. How did God prepare Moses to be such a great leader? It was through intimacy with Him. He spent forty years with God on the backside of a desert.

We live in a world where most don't want to spend forty minutes locked down with God in meditational prayer.

Intimacy with God comes not only through prayer but also worship. One of the joys and fulfilling times of my life as a preacher and pastor was when I went on my first missionary journey in 2007. Dr. Linda Marcell, the founder of Agape Global Mission, assembled a group of pastors to visit two nations on the continent of Africa. She had been serving in the mission field for quite some time, working with pastors and their churches in Kenya and Uganda. She asked us to help her by sharing our experience with many of the pastors in these countries. The team consisted of 5 pastors: the late Rev. Dr. David Larry Boyle, who pastored the Antioch Baptist Church in Whiteville, Tennessee (his topic was pastoral duties); Rev. Gary Faulkner, who is the pastor of the Cumming Street Baptist Church in Memphis, Tennessee (his topic was mission); Rev. Jerry Crisp, who is the pastor of the Union Hill Baptist Church in Whiteville, Tennessee (his topic was stewardship); Rev. Willie Ray Boyle, who is the pastor of the Home Baptist Church in Jackson, Tennessee (his topic was discipleship;) and I was blessed to be a part of the group and my topic of discussion being worship.

It was an experience that I will never forget. I had to teach and preach with an interpreter. The pastors sat in eager anticipation. I was being received with full acceptance of all that was being taught by the other members of the team and me. I took as many copies of my lesson plan on worship as I could take in my luggage because they were very limited in making copies. I gave a copy of the lesson plan to each of the pastors who attended the conferences and left the rest with the presidents of the Kenya and Uganda Baptist Ministerial Alliance to make copies once they could distribute them to others who could not attend the conference.

We were over there for about a month. I often think of when we got ready to return to the United States. They took five chairs and lined them up in front of where we were assembled. They had us all to sit down, and then they gathered around us, praying earnestly with much fervency giving thanks to God for sending us to them, praying that we would have a safe return home, and then they pleaded in prayer that we would return. To this day, I think about their prayer for us to return to them.

THROUGH PRAYER, WE PRAISE OUR MIGHTY GOD

I will thank you, Lord, with all my heart; I will tell of all the marvelous things you have done. I will be filled with joy because of you. I will sing praises to your name, O Most High.

Psalms 9:1-2

Praise is expressing to God our appreciation and understanding of His worth. It is saying thank you for each aspect of His divine nature. Our inward attitude becomes outward expression. Do you ever tell Him that there is none like Him? He loves to be told about Himself. You know how it makes you feel when someone says nice things about you or your family. Well, it is the same with Him, but on a larger scale. We don't properly understand being made in God's image and His likeness. We know how we are affected when treated a certain way, but we separate it when it comes to God, and we shouldn't. A good way to think of God is by seeing Him as you see yourself but without sin. You can be moved upon by praise, and so can God. One of the great examples of the power of praise is given in the Word of God.

2 Chronicles 20:1-22

Later, the Moabites, Ammonites, and some of the Meunites came to wage war against Jehoshaphat. Some men reported to Jehoshaphat, 'A large crowd is coming against you from the other side of the Dead Sea, from Edom. The crowd is already in Hazazon Tamar' (also called En Gedi). Frightened, Jehoshaphat decided to ask for the LORD'S help. He announced a fast throughout Judah. The people of Judah gathered to seek the LORD'S help. They came from every city in Judah. In the new courtyard at the LORD'S temple, Jehoshaphat stood in front of the people. He said, 'LORD God of our ancestors, aren't you the God in heaven? You rule all the kingdoms of the nations. You possess power and might, and no one can oppose you. Didn't you, our God, force those who were living in this country out of Israel's way? Didn't you give this country to the descendants of your friend Abraham to have permanently? His descendants have lived in it and built a holy temple in your name in it. They said, If evil comes in the form of war, flood, plague, or famine, we will stand in front of this temple and in front of you because your name is in this temple. We will cry out to you in our troubles, and you will hear us and save us. The Ammonites, Moabites, and the people of Mount Seir have come here. However, you didn't let Israel invade them when they came out of Egypt. The Israelites turned away from them and didn't destroy them. They are now paying us back by coming to force us out of the land that you gave to us. You're our God. Won't you judge them? We don't have the strength to face this large crowd that is attacking us. We don't know what to do, so we're looking to you.' All the people from Judah, their infants, wives, and children, were standing in front of the LORD. Then the LORD'S Spirit came to Jahaziel. (He was the son of Zechariah, grandson of Benaiah, great-grandson of Jeiel, whose father was Mattaniah, a Levite descended from Asaph.) Jahaziel said, 'Pay attention to me, everyone from Judah, everyone living in Jerusalem, and King Jehoshaphat. This is what the LORD says to you: Don't be frightened or terrified by this large crowd. The battle isn't yours. It's God's. Tomorrow goes into battle against them. They will be coming up the Ziz Pass. You will find them at the end of the valley in front of the Jeruel Desert. You won't fight this battle. {Instead,} take your position, standstill, and see the victory of the LORD for you, Judah, and Jerusalem. Don't be frightened or terrified. Tomorrow goes out to face them. The LORD is with you.' Jehoshaphat bowed down with his face touching the ground. Everyone from Judah and the people who lived in Jerusalem immediately bowed down in front of the LORD. The Levites, descendants of Kohath and Korah, stood up to praise the LORD God of Israel with very loud songs. They got up early in the morning and went to the desert of Tekoa. As they were leaving, Jehoshaphat stopped and said, 'Listen to me, people of Judah and those living in Jerusalem. Trust the LORD your God, and believe. Believe his prophets, and you will succeed.' After he had advised the people, he appointed people to sing to the LORD and praise him for the beauty of his holiness. As they went in front of the troops, they sang, 'Thank the LORD because his mercy endures forever!' As they started to sing praises, the LORD set ambushes against the Ammonites, Moabites, and the people of Mount Seir who had come into Judah. They were defeated.

Now we are to especially take note of when God took action; it was when the people started to praise. When we praise God, we help ourselves by expanding our awareness of who He is. In each psalm you read, look for an attribute or characteristic of God for which you can thank Him. It is good to thank the Lord and sing praises to the Most High. It is good to proclaim your unfailing love in the morning and your faithfulness in the evening. The challenge to be faithful is throughout the day and not when you go to bed at night; therefore, pray in the morning. During the Thanksgiving holiday, we focus on our blessings and express our gratitude to God for them. But thanks should be on our lips every day and throughout the day. We can never say thank you enough to parents, friends, leaders, and especially God. When Thanksgiving becomes an integral part of your life, you will find that your attitude toward life will change. You will become more positive, gracious, loving, and humble.

Know that when something is integral, it is very important because everything else works off of it. When I worked at Dover Corporation Elevator Company, I was given a blueprint to assemble a part called the integral header. I knew everything had to be within 1/64 of an inch in measurement. We had to assemble it without it being off any more than that. I had many of them returned to me after inspection for correction. I remember getting very upset at some of them being off no more than that; therefore, I asked for an explanation as to why they were so strict. I was told that everything works off of it; that all the other parts of the elevator worked off the integral header. In other words, if it was off, then nothing else would work right. Therefore it is crucial that we meet God early in the morning, beginning the day with Him because everything else works off of Him. Never fail to give God praise.

THE BIBLICAL WAY TO PRAY

Does the Bible teach a "right way" to pray? Yes, it does. We all have resorted to the Lord's Prayer in Matthew chapter 6 as an example of prayer. It is called "The Model Prayer." Parents teach it to their children early in life, it is used in worship services by way of a chant, and it is memorized by most. Hardly is there anyone who does not know or hasn't heard of the Lord's Prayer, but much prayer happened before Jesus came on the scene. It was very interesting that in my study on prayer, the Lord led me to what the Bible teaches in Nehemiah as an example of the right way to pray. Throughout the Bible, effective prayer includes elements of adoration, confession, commitment, and requests. Note that requests are last, but most people make it first.

Nehemiah 1:2-11
One of my brothers, Hanani, arrived with

some men from Judah. I asked them about the Jews who had survived captivity and about Jerusalem. They told me, 'Those who survived captivity are in the province. They are enduring serious troubles and being insulted. The wall of Jerusalem has been broken down, and its gates have been destroyed by fire.' When I heard this, I sat down and cried. I mourned for days. I continued to fast and pray to the God of heaven. I said, 'LORD God of heaven, great and awe-inspiring God, you faithfully keep your promise and show mercy to those who love you and obey your commandments. Open your eyes, and pay close attention with your ears to what I, your servant, am praying. I am praying to you day and night about your servants, the Israelites. I confess the sins that we Israelites have committed against you as well as the sins that my father's family and I have committed. We have done you a great wrong. We haven't obeyed the commandments, laws, or regulations that you gave us through your servant Moses. Please remember what you told us through your servant Moses: 'If you are unfaithful, I will scatter you among the nations. But if you return to me and continue to obey my commandments, though your people may be driven to the most distant point on the horizon, I will come and get you from there and bring you to the place where I chose to put my name.' These are your servants and your people whom you have saved by your great power and your strong hand. Lord, please pay attention to my prayer and to the prayers of all your other servants who want to worship your name. Please give me success today and make this man, King Artaxerxes, show me compassion.' I was cupbearer to the king at this time.

Nehemiah was deeply grieved about the condition of Jerusalem, but he didn't just brood about it. After his initial grief, he prayed, pouring his heart out to God. He looked for ways to improve the situation. In studying Nehemiah's prayer, I discovered that it directly opposes the understanding that most have of prayer, which is that you put it in God's hands and leave it there. That is to say that you pray and go on about your business. I opened the floor for discussion in Bible study over the above statement. I did that because I learned from a course at the American Baptist College entitled "Teaching for Results" by Finnly B. Edge that a good teacher does not do a monologue when he teaches but welcomes questions from the class. And if no one in the class asks questions, the teacher creates a dialogue by putting a question on the floor. He says we must do this because when you do a monologue, you do all the talking, and the people's minds grow closed. But when you ask a question, their minds become open because they are thinking, and that is when you can put something in their hearts. He says a teacher is teaching when someone says, "Hmmm...I see." We were taught that people teach themselves and the teacher is just a guide.

When the disciples of Rehoboth Baptist Church were told that you don't put a prayer in God's hand and leave it there, it generated a lot of discussions. We spent over a month on that one thought because everyone was getting involved and making it a real learning experience. One faithful disciple of the church named Sister Willie B. Springfield argued vehemently over what she had been taught all her life, which is when you pray, "You put it in God's hands and leave it there." She was shown that genuine prayer is keeping it before God.

Often, the problems we encounter that bring us to prayer are for God to get our minds. I have learned that God wants your thought life. He wants your mind to stay on Him. We love God with our minds (Matt. 22:37). Nehemiah didn't just put the problem he was facing in God's hands; he cried day and night unto the Lord, which is not putting it in God's hands and leaving it there. That is keeping it before God. That is walking in meditation with God, thinking and keeping your thoughts on Him. During our Bible Study, Ms. Willie B. Springfield created a discussion that helped everybody in the class. She argued what she had heard all her life. I showed her what Nehemiah did. He cried night and day unto God. Though she and others had a hard time accepting it, they could see, from the Word of God, that crying unto God night and day was not putting it in His hands and leaving it there. Then the Spirit led me to say to all present that if you forget about it, you are saying to God that your request is not very important, and He will treat it as such.

Prayer is not just for us to receive from God but for God to get his hands on us so that He can transform our lives. He is the potter, and we are the clay. The clay has to stay in the potter's hands for Him to do anything with it (Isaiah. 64:8). This is why God has to hold off on answering our prayers; because He knows the minute He answers us, we will be gone giving our minds right back to the concern of the flesh. We must know that God cannot be hired to answer our prayers. He is not on our payroll, that we can pray to Him and then forget about it. I learned that if you forget about it, He lays it aside until you return to spend time with Him.

Nehemiah gives us the proper order in prayer. In his prayer, he adores God, saying He is a great and awesome God who keeps His covenant of unfailing love with those who love Him and obey His commands. We are to let God know that we understand how He is, and then we are to confess our shortcomings, calling upon God to remember what He has said. We can do this according to what Solomon prayed.

Therefore now, LORD, let the thing that thou hast spoken concerning thy servant and concerning his house be established forever, and do as thou hast said.

1 Chronicles 17:23

Prayer is reminding God what He has said. Charles Spurgeon says God is insulted when we don't remind Him of what He has said. We must let God know who we are and what He has done for us as Nehemiah. He says to God that they are His servants, the people He rescued by His great power and might. He knew the king's heart was in God's hand, and He (God) could turn it as the rivers of waters. (Proverbs. 21:1)

Nehemiah put all his knowledge, experience, and organizational resources into determining what should be done. When tragic news comes to you, first pray. Then seek ways to move beyond grief to specific action that helps those who need it. He worked with God. Nehemiah fasted and prayed for several days, expressing his sorrow for Israel's sin and his desire that Jerusalem would again come alive with the worship of the one true God. Nehemiah demonstrated the elements of effective prayer. His concern was not for himself but for God, that he would be benefited. The elements of effective prayer are:

- Adoration
- Confession
- Intercession
- Recognition

- Commitment
- Request
- Supplication

Note again where requests and supplications are; they are last, but we have made them the first and only thing we do. Heartfelt prayers like Nehemiah's can help clarify any problem you may be facing, and God's great power will help you accomplish the job you have to do. By the end of his prayer, Nehemiah knew what action he had to take. (Nehemiah 1:11) When God's people pray, difficult decisions fall into proper perspective, and appropriate actions follow.

PRAYER IS TO BE SPONTANEOUS

The King asked, "Well, how can I help you?" With a prayer to the God of heaven, I replied, "If it pleases Your Majesty and if you are pleased with me, your servant, then send me to Judah to rebuild the city where my ancestors are buried.

Nehemiah 2:4

With little time to think, Nehemiah immediately prayed. He was praying through mental thought while the King was talking to him. He did not wait until he was alone or that night when he went to bed to pray. He prayed right there and then. God is listening according to the Word of God.

And it shall come to pass, that before they call, I will answer; and while they are yet speaking, I will hear.

Isaiah 65:24

A Prayer of the afflicted, when he is overwhelmed, and poured out his complaint before the LORD. Hear my prayer, O LORD, and let my cry come unto thee. Hide not thy face from me in the day when I am in trouble; incline thine ear unto me: in the day when I call answer me speedily.

Psalm 102:1-2

I know now that prayer is spending time with God. That is the reason if you are a child of God as to why trouble comes into your life. David says in Psalm 119:67, "Before I was afflicted I went astray, but now have I kept thy word."

It is good for me that I have been afflicted, that I might learn thy statutes.

Psalm 119:71

I know, O LORD, that thy judgments are right, and that thou in faithfulness hast afflicted me.

Psalm 119:75

I had to accept this like David. God introduces Himself to us through our trials and tribulations. If you don't stay with God as He takes you through something, you will never know God; you will only know of Him. Eight times in the book of Nehemiah, you read where he prayed spontaneously.

Then the king said unto me, for what dost thou make request? So I prayed to the God of heaven.

Nehemiah 2:4

Hear, O our God; for we are despised: turn their reproach upon their own head, and give them for a prey in the land of captivity: And cover not their iniquity, and let not their sin be blotted out from before thee: for they have provoked thee to anger before the builders.

Nehemiah 4:4-5

Nevertheless we made our prayer unto our God, and set a watch against them day and night, because of them.

Nehemiah 4:9

Think upon me, my God, for good, according to all that I have done for this people.

Nehemiah 5:19

My God, think thou upon Tobiah and Sanballat according to these their works, and on the prophetess Noadiah, and the rest of the prophets, that would have put me in fear.

Nehemiah 6:14

Remember me, O my God, concerning this, and wipe not out my good deeds that I have done for the house of my God, and for the offices thereof.

Nehemiah 13:14

And I commanded the Levites that they should cleanse themselves, and that they should come and keep the gates, to sanctify the Sabbath day. Remember me, O my God, concerning this also, and spare me according to the greatness of thy mercy.

Nehemiah 13:22

Remember them, O my God, because they have defiled the priesthood, and the covenant of the priesthood, and of the Levites.

Nehemiah 13:29

Nehemiah prayed at any time, even while talking with others. He knew that God was always listening. God is in charge, always present, and hears and answers every prayer. Nehemiah could confidently pray throughout the day because he had established an intimate relationship with God during extended prayer. (Nehemiah 1:4-7) If we want to reach God with our emergency prayers, we need to take time to cultivate a strong relationship with God through times of in-depth prayer. In-depth prayer is not what one might think it is, i.e., lengthy with all the right words. In-depth prayer is as constant as breathing. God is in your thoughts as breath is in your body.

You might want to say that you won't have time for yourself if you think of God that much. What *self*? Remember, you don't belong to yourself. You have been bought with a price. If you are truly saved, you are dead through the death, burial, and resurrection of our Lord, who also ascended and will return. *Self* died when you accepted Christ. You are a new creature, remember? Spontaneous praying is mentally carrying it to God in your thought life when you are made aware of something and need God's intervention. So it was with Nehemiah and also Hannah.

Now Hannah spoke in her heart; only her lips moved, but her voice was not heard. Therefore Eli thought she had been drunken.

1 Samuel 1:13

I encourage all to make it a habit of spontaneously carrying everything to God in prayer, for He promises, "And it shall come to pass, that before they call, I will answer; and while they are yet speaking, I will hear.

Isaiah 65: 24

But when he saw the wind boisterous, he was afraid; and beginning to sink, he cried, saying, Lord, save me. And immediately Jesus stretched forth his hand, and caught him, and said unto him, O thou of little faith, wherefore didst thou doubt? And when they were come into the ship, the wind ceased.

Matthew 14:30-32

These scriptures give us a perfect example of spontaneous prayer. Sinking times are praying times with the Lord's servants. Peter neglected prayer upon starting his venturous journey, but when he began to sink, his danger made him suppliant, and his cry, although late, was not too late. In our hours of bodily pain and mental anguish, we find ourselves as naturally driven to prayer as the wreck is driven upon the shore by the waves. The fox hides in its hole for protection, the bird flies to the wood for shelter, and even so, the tried believer hastens to the mercy seat for safety. Heaven's great harbor of refuge is prayer. Thousands of weather-beaten vessels have found a haven there, and the moment a storm comes on, it is wise for us to make for it with all sail.

Short prayers are long enough. There were but three words in the petition which Peter gasped out, but they were sufficient for his purpose. Not length, but strength is desirable. A sense of need is a mighty teacher of brevity. If our prayers had less of the tail feathers of pride and more wings of humility, they would be all the better. Verbiage is to devotion as chaff is to wheat. Precious things lie in small compass, and all that is real prayer in many a long address might have been uttered in a petition as short as Peter's.

Our extremities are the Lord's opportunities. Immediately a keen sense of danger forces an anxious cry from us. The ear of Jesus hears, and with Him, the ear and heart go together, and the hand does not long linger. At the last moment, we appeal to our Master, but His swift hand makes up for our delays with instant and effectual action. Are we nearly engulfed by the boisterous waters of affliction? Let us then lift our souls unto our Savior, and we may rest assured that He will not suffer us to perish. When we can do nothing, and Jesus can do all things, let us enlist His powerful aid upon our side, and all will be well.

JESUS' TEACHING ON PRAYER

If there ever was one who knew the value of prayer, it was our spotless, perfect Lord Jesus Christ. None was ever so much in supplication as He! Such was His love for His Father that He loved to be in communion with Him. Such was His love for His people that He desired to be much in intercession for them. This eminent prayerfulness of Jesus is a lesson for us—He has given us an example that we may follow in His steps. The time He chose was admirable; it was early in the morning. Mark records in his gospel in Mark 1:35: "*And in the morning, rising up a great while before day, he went out, and departed into a solitary place, and there prayed.*" He chose an hour when all was quiet. There is no better time to pray than when all is quiet. Jesus got away from the crowd so that He would not be disturbed. While others found rest in sleep, He refreshed Himself with prayer.

The place was also well selected. It was a solitary place. Those dark and silent hills were a fit atmosphere for the Son of God. Heaven and earth, in midnight stillness, heard the groans and sighs of the mysterious Being in whom both worlds were blended. The continuance of His pleadings is remarkable. The long watches were not too long. The cold wind did not chill His devotions. The grim darkness did not darken His faith. Loneliness did not check His persistence. It was shown to us by the disciples that we cannot watch with Him for one hour, but He watches for us all the time.

The occasion for this prayer of Jesus was notable; it was after His enemies had been enraged. Prayer was His refuge and solace. It was before He sent forth the twelve apostles. Prayer was the gate of His endeavor, the courier of His new work. Should we not learn from Jesus to resort to special prayer when we are under peculiar trials or contemplating fresh activities for the Master's glory? Lord Jesus, teach us to pray. Jesus taught His disciples that prayer is an intimate relationship with the Father that includes a dependency for daily needs and commitment to obedience and forgiveness of sin (Matthews 6:5-13).

And when you pray, don't be like the hypocrites who love to pray publicly on street corners and in the synagogues where everyone can see them. I assure you that is all the reward they will ever get.

Matthew 6:5

There is a proper attitude that goes along with prayer. A story is told of this pastor who went to a certain city to pastor a church. There were many churches in this city, and they fellowshipped with each other. There were two men in the community that were known as great prayers. The people loved to hear them pray in the church, so much so that there would be requests for them to pray. They were members of different churches, one was a Methodist, and the other was a Baptist, but they visited each other's churches. They both were eloquent prayers from the people's perspective, although it was basically memorized prayer. Even the pastors in the community talked about how they could pray. When they ended up at the same church together, they wouldn't pray, although that was what the people wanted.

Jesus said, "But when you pray go away by yourself, shut the door behind you, and pray to your Father secretly. Then your Father, who knows all secrets, will reward you openly."

Matthew 6:6

Prayer is not all about us; it is about God and getting His attention, although He is always thinking of us. Getting God's attention while He is thinking about us sounds like an oxymoron. The point is to get Him involved in your situation while He thinks of you.

How precious also are thy thoughts unto me.

Psalms 139:17

David is not alarmed at the fact that God knows all about him; on the contrary, he is comforted and even feels himself to be enriched, as though he has a chest of precious jewels. That God should think upon him is the believer's treasure and pleasure. He cries,

"How costly, how valued are thy thoughts, how dear to me is thy perpetual attention!" He thinks upon God's thoughts with delight. The more of them, the better He is pleased. It is a joy worth words that the Lord should think of us who are so poor and needy. It is a joy that fills our whole nature to think upon God, returning love for love, thought for thought, after our poor fashion. When we remember that God's thoughts are upon us from all eternity, He continues to think upon us every moment, and He will think of us when time shall be no more, we may well exclaim, "How great is the sum!" Note what the Psalmist says about God's thoughts of us.

How precious also are thy thoughts unto me, O God! How great is the sum of them! If I should count them, they are more in number than the sand: when I awake, I am still with thee.

Psalms 139:17-18

Many, O LORD my God, are thy wonderful works which thou hast done, and thy thoughts which are to us-ward: they cannot be reckoned up in order unto thee: if I would declare and speak of them, they are more than can be numbered.

Psalms 40:5

Thoughts such as are natural to the Creator, the Preserver, the Redeemer, the Father, and the Friend are evermore flowing from the Lord. Thoughts of our pardon, renewal, upholding, supplying, educating, perfecting, and a thousand more kinds perpetually well up in the mind of the Most High. It should fill us with adoring wonder and reverent surprise that the infinite mind of God should turn so many thoughts toward us when we are so insignificant and unworthy!

This is why a proper understanding of prayer is needed. Your thought life is a form of prayer. Shall he think so much of us and we so little of Him? Have you ever called somebody and they said to you that they were just thinking about you? How does it make you feel? Well, think of God in the same fashion, purposing in your heart to not let the things of the world crowd the Lord out of your mind but spend much time with Him. I guarantee that no one can give you as satisfying a peace as He can. I tell you, you will grow to delight in God. This greatly contrasts the notion of those who deny the existence of a personal, conscious God.

Imagine a world without a thinking, personal God! Conceive of a grim providence of machinery! A fatherhood of law! Such philosophy is hard and cold, but to have a God always thinking of us makes a happy world, a rich life, and a heavenly hereafter. In Matthew 6:7, Jesus taught His disciples, "When you pray, don't babble on and on as people of other religions do. They think their prayers are answered only by repeating their words again and again. Don't be like them, because your Father knows exactly what you need even before you ask Him!" What is He after since He knows? He is after your mind, your thoughts.

He wants your attention on Him. We are to love God with all our heart, soul, mind, and strength.

Matthew 6:9-13 tells us that Jesus told His disciples to pray like this, "Our Father in heaven, may your name be honored. May your Kingdom come. May your will be done here on earth, as it is in heaven. Give us our food for today and forgive us our sins, just as we have forgiven those who have sinned against us. And don't let us yield to temptation, but deliver us from the evil one."

Some people, especially religious leaders, wanted to be seen as holy, and public prayer was one way to get attention. Jesus saw through their self-righteous acts, and He can see through ours. He taught that the essence of prayer is not public style but private communication with God. There is a place for public prayer, but to pray only where others will notice you indicate that your real audience is not God.

Just as the story told earlier about the Baptist and Methodist prayers, if you are not careful, your audience may not be God but the people. Repeating the same words over and over like a magic incantation is no way to ensure that God will hear your prayer, although it's not wrong to come to God many times with the same requests. Jesus encourages persistent prayer. But He condemns the shallow repetition of words not offered with a sincere heart.

What determines a sincere heart? It is a heart that communes with God throughout the day. It is the heart that is on God all while you are doing your other work. Believe me. It doesn't interfere with your other work. On the contrary, it makes it go better. I can remember the secular job I worked at Dover Corporation. I was given a blueprint to assemble a particular part of the elevator. I could read the blueprint and assemble the part per specification, all while I communed with God. Many times, I would get so caught up with God that tears would roll down my face like sweat. When I went full-time in the ministry, the person working in the next station told me that he saw me crying many times while I was working and wondered what was happening. I told him that I was talking to God.

One particular time, God was giving me the sermon for that upcoming Sunday. I stopped welding and took a notepad out of my pocket to write down what God was giving me. When I attended American Baptist College, our professor told us as preachers that when God comes to us, we must be ready to write it down, or we will forget it. My supervisor caught me writing one day instead of working on my job for the elevator company. I was still working but on my job for the Lord.

I was later told that my supervisor stood behind me for a long time before he said anything to me. Others saw him standing behind me, but I didn't know it. He finally said something. He asked me what I was doing. I told him that I was writing down something God gave me for Sunday's sermon. He calmly said, "You know you can't be doing that." Thank God that he was a Christian. Now, what generated me to stop my work, take out my notepad and jot down the dictates of the Holy Spirit? I asked this question one night in class about trying to remember what the Holy Spirit says to us while we are working, and we try to remember it once we get home. It had failed miserably with me. I had a spiritual nugget of pure gold that I couldn't recall when I got home that evening.

That was when our professor at American Baptist College told us as preachers to always carry a notepad with us because the Holy Spirit has no certain time that He will come to us. He can break in at any time while one is praying in thought.

We can never pray too much if our prayers are honest and sincere. Before you start to pray, make sure you mean what you say. What Jesus was teaching is often called the Lord's Prayer because Jesus gave it to the disciples. It can be a pattern for our prayers. We should praise God, pray for His work in the world, pray for our daily needs, and pray for help in our daily struggles.

The phrase *Our Father in heaven* indicates that God is not only majestic and holy but also personal and loving. The first line of this model prayer is a statement of praise and a commitment to hallow, or honor, God's holy name. We can honor God's name by being careful to use it respectfully. If we use God's name lightly, we aren't remembering God's holiness. I once had a habit of saying, "*Lord have mercy,*" when someone would tell me something that happened to another that wasn't pleasant. I would automatically say, "*Lord have mercy,*" out of habit, and I wasn't even thinking about God. I know now that I must have my thoughts on Him. Otherwise, I am taking His name in vain.

"*May your kingdom come soon*" refers to God's spiritual reign, not Israel's freedom from Rome. God's Kingdom was announced in the covenant with Abraham and is now present in Christ's reign in believers' hearts. It will be complete when all evil is destroyed, and God establishes the new heaven and earth. (Revelation 21:1) When we pray, "*May your will be done,*" we are not resigning ourselves to fate. We are praying that God's perfect purpose will be accomplished in this world and the next. When we pray, "*Give us our food for today,*" we are acknowledging that God is our sustainer and provider. It is a misconception to think that we provide for ourselves. We must trust God daily to provide what He knows we need. The prayer is a model and is not necessarily to be prayed.

God sometimes allows us to be tested by temptation. As disciples, we should pray to be delivered from these trying times and for deliverance from Satan ("the evil one") and his deceit. All Christians struggle with temptation. Sometimes it is so subtle that we don't even realize what is happening to us. God has promised that He won't allow us to be tempted beyond what we can bear. (1 Corinthians 10:13) Ask God to help you recognize temptation and to give you strength to overcome and choose God's way instead.

BE CONSISTENT AND PERSISTENT

Contrary to popular opinion, prayer is not putting it in God's hands and leaving it there. This point was made very clear to the disciples of Rehoboth Baptist Church regarding the parable of Jesus' teaching that proper praying is not putting it in His hand and leaving it there but continually keeping it before God. Jesus told his disciples a parable to illustrate their need for constant prayer and to show them that they must never give up.

Luke 18:1-8

There was a judge in a certain city," he said, "Who was a godless man with great contempt for everyone. A widow of that city came to him repeatedly, appealing for justice against someone who had harmed her. The judge ignored her for a while, but eventually she wore him down. I fear neither God nor man,' he said to himself,' but this woman is driving me crazy. I'm going to see that she gets justice, because she is wearing me out with her constant requests!'" Then the Lord said, "Learn a lesson from this evil judge. Even he rendered a just decision in the end, so don't you think God will surely give justice to his chosen people who plead with him day and night? I tell you, he will grant justice to them quickly! But when I, the Son of Man, return, how many will I find who have faith?

Crying day and night doesn't look like putting it in God's hands and leaving it there. On the contrary, it's more like keeping it before God in thought, praying constantly. Concerning the unjust judge, will he keep putting them off? To persist in prayer does not mean endless repetition or painfully long prayer sessions. Constant prayer means keeping our requests before God as we live for Him daily, believing He will answer. When we live by faith, we are not to give up. God may delay answering, but his delays always have good reasons. As we persist in prayer, we grow in character, faith, and hope.

Prayer has a double role, but most only see it as having one role, and that is for us to receive from God. However, prayer is for God to be able to transform your life. If He doesn't have your thought life, He doesn't have you. This is why He may hold off on answering our prayers. He knows the minute you get your answer, you are gone. We take ourselves out of His hand by giving our thoughts to something else, and most of the time, it's something worldly. Jesus gives us another example of the power of prayer in the gospel of Luke.

Luke 11:5-13

Jesus said to his disciples,' Suppose one of you has a friend. Suppose you go to him at midnight and say, "Friend, let me borrow three loaves of bread. A friend of mine on a trip has dropped in on me, and I don't have anything to serve him." Your friend might answer you from inside his house, "Don't bother me! The door is already locked, and my children are in bed. I can't get up to give you anything." I can guarantee that although he doesn't want to get up to give you anything, he will get up and give you whatever you need because he is your friend and because you were so bold. So I tell you to ask, and you will receive. Search, and you will find. Knock, and the door will be opened for you. Everyone who asks will receive. The one who searches will find, and for the person who knocks, the door will be opened. If your child asks you, his father, for a fish, would you give him a snake instead? Or if your child asks you for an egg, would you give him a scorpion? Even though you're evil, you know how to give good gifts to your children. So how much more will your Father in heaven give the Holy Spirit to those who ask him?

Persistence or boldness in prayer overcomes our insensitivity, not God's. Practicing persistence does more for us. It does more to change our hearts and minds than God's, and it helps us understand and express the intensity of our needs. Persistence in prayer helps us recognize God's work. If the godless judges responded to constant pressure, how much more would a great and loving God respond to us? If we know He loves us, we can believe He will hear our cries for help. We are told in Luke 18:8, "*He will grant justice to them quickly! But when I, the Son of Man, return, how many will I find who have faith?*"

Look at what waiting does. He stretches our faith by waiting to answer our prayers. Through my experience in life, He has made me a man of faith. I didn't know then that this was what He was doing, but I'm glad He did. Permit me to enlarge upon an experience I alluded to when I went full-time, and the church would not increase my salary.

I sank into debt, and what was once good credit became bad. When I had good credit, if I went somewhere and wanted to buy something, all I had to do was just call the bank, and they would speak to the merchant; the merchant would let me have what I wanted, and the loan officer would fix the papers up later. I remember one time I needed another car, so I went to Jackson, Tennessee, and upon finding the car I wanted, that was what I did. I was before that same person in a very bad fix, and he turned me down. My once good name with the bank was destroyed. I had to be persistent in prayer.

The bank where we did business was preparing to foreclose on our home. We were at risk of losing everything we had. My wife and I prayed that it wouldn't happen, and we were being persistent. I went into the bank and asked for a loan to keep my property. I said to the loan officer, "You know me! You know I will pay you back!"

He said to me, "Patrick, I know how you once were when you were working at Dover and serving at the church, but now you are just serving at the church. Your credit is bad." So he turned us down. I left the bank and went and told my wife. I embraced her and cried, and she cried too. But we kept praying, and once we somewhat composed ourselves, I heard the voice of God tell me to go back to the bank and talk to the loan officer again. I was reluctant but obedient. I went back to the bank. I went in, and he had someone else in his office. He looked out and saw me waiting to see him again. When his other customer left, I got up, walked to his door, and asked to see him again. He told me to come in, and I said, "I know you told me you couldn't do it, but the Lord sent me back to you."

He paused, then shook his head and said, "Patrick, I don't see how you will pay us back, but I'm going to let you have it." The loan officer, Mr. Larry Childers, had to leave the bank for issuing that loan. But the Lord blessed him to go into his own business, Childers Real Estate, and he is doing well to this day. He obeyed the voice of God and God rewarded him!

DOES GOD ALWAYS ANSWER PRAYER?

We can be confident of God's response to our prayers when we submit first to His will.

James 5:13-18

Are any among you suffering? They should keep on praying about it. And those who have reason to be thankful should continually sing praises to the Lord. Are any among you sick? They should call for the elders of the church and have them pray over them, anointing them with oil in the name of the Lord. And their prayer offered in faith will heal the sick, and the Lord will make them well. And anyone who has committed sins will be forgiven. Confess your sins to each other and pray for each other so that you may be healed. The earnest prayer of a righteous person has great power and wonderful results. Elijah was as human as we are, yet when he prayed earnestly that no rain would fall, none fell for the next three and a half years! Then he prayed for rain, and down it poured. The grass turned green, and the crops began to grow again.

Verse 17 says he prayed earnestly. The word earnestly is characterized by or proceeding from an intense state of mind, a serious mental state. Although the early Christians had access to and freely used the Old Testament, they did not yet have the New Testament or any other Christian books to study. Their stories and teachings about Christ were memorized and passed on from person to person. Sometimes the teachings were set to music, so music became an important part of Christian worship and education.

This is why certain songs should not be sung. There is a song that says, "*I don't need nobody as long as I got Jesus.*" The song can be misleading when it comes to church attendance. We do need others. This is why Hebrews 10:25 tells us, "*Not forsaking the assembling of ourselves together, as the manner of some is; but exhorting one another, and so much the more, as ye see the day approaching.*" We are not to forsake the assembling of ourselves together; we are strength to one another. In a day of affliction, nothing is more seasonable than prayer. The person afflicted must pray himself, as well as engage the prayers of others for him.

People ask me all the time to pray for them. I now ask them, "Are you praying for yourself?" Times of affliction should be praying times. In some cases, the *prayer offered in faith* does not refer to the faith of the sick person but to the faith of the people praying. God heals. Faith doesn't. And all prayers are subject to God's will. But prayer is part of God's healing process. I John 5: 14-15, tells us that we can be confident that He will listen to us whenever we ask Him for anything in line with His will.

If you abide in me and my Word abides in you, you can ask what you will and it shall be done for you.

John 15:7

It has been revealed to me that this is not material things, as most want to believe. Now this is preached and taught by many, and it is called the prosperity gospel. I have come to understand that if you are abiding in Him and His Word is abiding in you, which means you are controlled by His Word, you will only ask for that which honors Him, i.e., spiritual things. Therefore this confidence doesn't make void the need to be persistent or to pray in the will of God. He promises to answer when we pray according to His will.

The word *will* is in the Greek present subjunctive mood, which refers to continuous repeated action without implying anything about the time of the action. 1 John 5:15 says, "*And if we know He is listening when we make our requests, we can be sure that He will give us what we ask for.*" The emphasis here is on praying in *God's will*, not our own. When we communicate with God, we don't demand what we want but discuss what He wants for us. The popular notion of "*name it and claim it*" doesn't work with God. We must adhere to God's word.

Trust the LORD with all your heart, and do not rely on your own understanding. In all your ways, acknowledge Him, and He will make your paths smooth. Do not consider yourself wise. Fear the LORD, and turn away from evil. {Then} your body will be healed, and your bones will have nourishment. Honor the LORD with your wealth and with the first and best part of all your income. Then your barns will be full, and your vats will overflow with fresh wine. Do not reject the discipline of the LORD, my son, and do not resent His warning, because the LORD warns the one He loves, even as a father warns a son with whom he is pleased.

Proverbs 3:5-12

When we align our prayers to His will, He will listen. Then we can be certain that if He listens, He will give us a definite answer. Therefore start praying with confidence! We must find our situation in scripture and pray according to what is written. What is written is His will. An example is the case of Jesus healing the woman who had the issue of blood for twelve years. When praying about sickness, we should remind God that He heals people who come to Him in faith. Remind Him of His healing of Hezekiah, who turned his faith to the wall and reminded God how he had lived. I know now that when you search the scripture for your situation, God will often not let you immediately find your situation. As you search the scripture, you will be shown yourself and led to a lot of confessing and repenting. Then He will allow you to find your particular situation. To this end, God sends afflictions that we may be engaged to seek Him early; and that those who at other times have neglected Him may be brought to enquire after Him. The spirit is humble, the heart is broken and tender, and prayer is most acceptable to God when it comes from a contrite, humble spirit.

The righteous cry and the LORD hears, and delivers them out of all their troubles.

Psalm 34:17

Like Israel in Egypt, they cry out under the heavy yoke of oppression, sin, temptation, care, and grief. God is like the night watchman, who no sooner hears the alarm bell than flies to relieve those who need him. No amount of trouble can so hold us that the Lord cannot free us. Our afflictions may be numerous and complicated, but prayer can free us from them all, for the Lord will show himself strong on our behalf. Psalm 34:18 says, "The LORD is nigh unto them that are of a broken heart; and saves such as be of a contrite spirit." I have been shown, and let me pass it on to you, that

God is big on His children having a contrite heart.

The sacrifices of God are a broken spirit: a broken and a contrite heart, O God, thou wilt not despise.

Psalm 51:17

For thus saith the high and lofty One that inhabited eternity, whose name is Holy; I dwell in the high and holy place, with him also that is of a contrite and humble spirit, to revive the spirit of the humble, and to revive the heart of the contrite ones.

Isaiah 57:15

Thus saith the LORD, The heaven is my throne, and the earth is my footstool: where is the house that ye build unto me, and where is the place of my rest? For all those things have mine hands made, and all those things have been, saith the LORD; but to this man will I look, even to him that is poor and of a contrite spirit, and trembled at my word.

Isaiah 66:1-2

God will be near in friendship to accept and console a contrite spirit. Far too many of God's children will not allow themselves to be broken. We think it is being weak when it actually is being strong. Broken hearts often think God is far away, but He is ever near. Some are so blind that they do not see their best friend. Indeed, He is with and in them, but they know it not. They run here and there, seeking peace in their works, or some experience they have had, or in proposals and resolutions, whereas the Lord is nigh them, and the simple act of faith will reveal Him. What a blessed token for good is a repentant, mourning heart! Just when the sinner condemns himself, the Lord graciously absolves him. If we chasten our spirits, the Lord will spare us. He will ease up with the rod of judgment on those already sore with the rod of conviction. Salvation is linked with contrition.

Many are the afflictions of the righteous, but the LORD delivered him out of them all.

Psalms 34:19

As a result, they are made like Jesus, their covenant Head. Scripture does not flatter us like the story books with the idea that goodness will secure us from trouble. On the contrary, we are repeatedly warned to expect tribulation while in this body. This I haven't always known, but I know it now. Our afflictions come from all points of the compass and are as many and as tormenting as nets are around something rotten. It is the earthly portion of the elect to find thorns and briars growing in their pathway and lie down among them, finding their rest broken and disturbed by sorrow. Oh, how it takes the sting out of the previous sentence! Jehovah God shall lead His redeemed unscathed and triumphant.

There is an end to the believer's affliction, a joyful end at that. None of his trials can hurt so much as a hair of his head; neither can the furnace hold him for a moment after the Lord bids him come out of it. Hard would be the lot of the righteous if this promise, like a bundle of campfire, were not bound up in it, but this sweetens it all. The same Lord who sends the afflictions will also recall them when His designs are accomplished, but He will never allow the fiercest of them to destroy His beloved. Afflictions will naturally draw out complaints.

Oh, how much and how often have I complained, and who do we complain to but God in prayer? It is necessary to exercise faith and hope under afflictions, and prayer is the appointed means to obtain and increase these graces in us. The Word says in James 5:13, "*Is any afflicted? Let him pray.*" Here it is again, prayer is not just for us to receive from God, but it positions us for God to work on us spiritually, giving us virtues and graces that we need in life.

Singing psalms is very proper and seasonable on a day of mirth and prosperity. We are urged to sing psalms, making melody in our hearts unto the Lord. There is a lot for us to learn from the writings of several in the first ages of Christianity. The older saints back in the 1950s on through the 1980s were accustomed to singing hymns, either taken out of scripture or out of more private composure in their worship of God, as I used to hear my mother doing as she walked around in that kitchen with one wood stove that was burning as she was cooking. Sadly, we are getting away from hymns and spiritual songs in our churches. Though some have thought that Paul's advice to both the Colossians and Ephesians to speak to one another in psalms, hymns, and spiritual songs refers only to the compositions of scripture, he was telling them to spend time talking with each other about the Psalms of David which was composed from the experience of David. Be that as it may, this we are sure of, the singing of psalms is a gospel ordinance, and our joy should be holy, consecrated to God.

Singing is so directed here to show that if we are in circumstances of mirth and prosperity, we should turn this mirth, though alone and by ourselves, into singing. Let our singing be such as to make melody with our hearts unto the Lord, and God will assuredly be well pleased with this kind of devotion. The melody of our heart is a form of prayer that has power with God but is unused by many children of God. Thank God for my wife! She uses this form of prayer a lot, especially when we are traveling. We cut everything off, and I just listened to the road and her making a melody in her heart to the Lord.

People in the church are not alone. Members of Christ's body should be able to count on others for support and prayer, especially when they are sick or suffering. The elders should be on call to respond to the illness of any member, and the church should be sensitive to the needs of all its members. If any be sick, they are required to send for the elders, the presbyters, pastors, or ministers of the church (James 5:14-15). It lies upon sick people as a duty to send for ministers and to desire their assistance and their prayers. It is the duty of ministers to pray over the sick when thus desired and called for. Let them pray over him; let their prayers be suited to the sick person's case, and their intercessions be as heartfelt as those affected by the calamities. In times of miraculous healing, the sick were to be anointed with oil in the name of the Lord. Expositors generally confine this anointing with oil to have the power to work miracles. When miracles ceased, this institution ceased also. We have doctors and hospitals to go to now when we get sick.

This is one thing that needs carefully to be observed here, that the saving of the sick is not ascribed to the anointing with oil, to the doctor or hospitals, but to prayer. The prayer of faith shall save the sick. Prayer over the sick must proceed from, and be accompanied by, a lively faith. There must be faith both in the person praying and the person being prayed for. In a time of sickness, it is not the cold and formal prayer that is effectual, but the prayer of faith. We should observe the success of prayer. The Lord shall raise him, and if he has committed sins, they shall be forgiven him; that is, where sickness is sent as a punishment for some particular sin, that sin shall be pardoned, and in token thereof, the sickness shall be removed.

When Christ said to the impotent man, "*Go and sin no more, lest a worse thing come unto thee,*" in John 5:14, it was clear that some particular sin was the cause of his sickness. Therefore, the pardoning of sin is the great thing we should beg of God for ourselves and others in times of sickness. Sin is both the root of sickness and the sting of it. If sin is pardoned, either affliction shall be removed in mercy, or we shall see there is mercy in the continuance of it. When healing is founded upon being pardoned, we may say as Hezekiah did in Isaiah 38:17, "*Thou have in love to my soul, delivered it from the pit of corruption.*" When you are sick and in pain, it is most common to pray and cry, "O give me ease, and restore me to health!" But your prayer should rather and chiefly be, "O that God would pardon my sins!" This perhaps poses a question to you as it did to me. Is all sickness because of sin? The answer is "No" because the same question was put to Jesus by the disciples.

And his disciples asked him, saying, Master, who did sin, this man, or his parents, that he was born blind.
John 9:2-3

Then Jesus gives a higher reason why the man was born blind. Jesus answered, "*Neither hath this man sinned, nor his parents but that the works of God should be made manifest in him.*" I wonder which of us have been chosen to become sick so that the works of God may be manifested. In Mark's gospel, we read of the apostles anointing many that were sick with oil and healing them (Mark 6:13). We have accounts of this being practiced in the church two hundred years after

Christ. But then the gift of healing also accompanied it, and when the miraculous gift ceased, this rite was laid aside. We said earlier that *"prayer offered in faith"* does not refer to the faith of the sick person but to the faith of the people praying. God heals, faith doesn't, and all prayers are subject to God's will, but prayer is part of God's healing process. Christians are directed to confess their faults to one another and pray with and for one another. Christ has made it possible for us to go directly to God for forgiveness. But confessing our sins to each other still has an important place in the church's life.

1. If we have sinned against an individual, we must ask him or her to forgive us.

2. If our sin has affected the church, we must confess it publicly.

What sins affect the church? There is an example in the scripture.

I Corinthians 5: 1-6

It is reported commonly that there is fornication among you, and such fornication as is not so much as named among the Gentiles, that one should have his father's wife. And ye are puffed up, and have not rather mourned, that he that hath done this deed might be taken away from among you. For I verily, as absent in body, but present in spirit, have judged already, as though I were present, concerning him that hath so done this deed. In the name of our Lord Jesus Christ, when ye are gathered together and my spirit, with the power of our Lord Jesus Christ to deliver such a one unto Satan for the destruction of the flesh that the spirit may be saved in the day of the Lord Jesus. Your glorying is not good. Know ye not that a little leaven leavened the whole lump?

I remember growing up as a child down on the Bass farm in Whiteville, Tennessee, and how Momma would make some homemade rolls (and she could make some good ones!). The way she made them was to put some yeast in some dough and let it set overnight, and it would spread all over the container. The next day she would make the rolls. If we need loving support as we struggle with sin, we should confess that sin to those who can provide that support. This can be God or an individual.

If we doubt God's forgiveness after confessing a sin to him, we may wish to confess that sin to a fellow believer for assurance of God's pardon. The scripture does say we are to confess our faults one to another. In Christ's Kingdom, every believer is a priest to other believers (1 Peter 2:9). It is understood by some that verse 16 is done in verse 14, as if when sick people send for ministers to pray over them, they should then confess their faults to them. Indeed where any are conscious that their sickness is a vindictive punishment of some particular sin, they cannot look for the removal of their sickness without particular applications to God for the pardon of such a sin. There it may be proper to acknowledge and tell his case, that those who pray over him may know how to plead rightly for him. But the confession here required is that of Christians to one another and not, as the Catholic would have it, to a priest. Where persons have injured one another, acts of injustice must be confessed to those against whom they have been committed. Where persons have tempted one another to sin or consented to the same evil actions, they ought mutually to blame themselves and encourage each other to repentance. Where crimes are of a public nature and have made public mischief, they ought to be more publicly confessed, so healing may best reach all concerned. And sometimes, it may be well to confess your faults to your pastor, some faithful minister you know, or a praying friend so that he may help you plead with God for mercy and pardon. Asking your pastor or another man of God is supported by scripture.

So Samuel called unto the LORD; and the LORD sent thunder and rain that day: and all the people greatly feared the LORD and Samuel. And all the people said unto Samuel, "Pray for thy servants unto the LORD thy God that we die not: for we have added unto all our sins this evil, to ask us a king.

I Samuel 12:18-19

And the king answered and said unto the man of God, 'Entreat now the face of the LORD thy God, and pray for me, that my hand may be restored me again.' And the man of God besought the LORD, and the king's hand was restored him again, and became as it was before.

I King 13:6

It is written in James 5:16, "*Confess your faults one to another, and pray one for another, that ye may be healed. The effectual fervent prayer of a righteous man avails much.*" In one carrying out what James says, we are not to think that James is indicating that we are to tell everything that we are conscious of that is amiss in ourselves or one another; but so far as confession is necessary to our reconciliation with those that are at odds with us, and for gaining information and making our spirits quiet and easy. Therefore, we should be ready to confess our faults.

I don't believe we need to go beyond what is necessary. For example, I knew a minister who believed he was to bring up and expose misdeeds that no one knew about but him and the person involved. The person was having a good life and a good marriage, but once the minister exposed the past life of this person, it destroyed the peace in this person's home. Though healing and deliverance can come to Christians in disclosing their peculiar weaknesses and infirmities to one another, it can only be done where there are great intimacies and friendships and where they may help each other by their prayers to obtain pardon of their sins and power against them. Those who confess their faults one to another should thereupon pray with and for one another. I think this is why we have the one to another understanding, to not have to disclose that which is going to destroy.

James 5:13 directs persons to pray for themselves, "Is any afflicted, let him pray." James 5:14 gives direction to seek the prayers of ministers. And James 5:16 directs private Christians to pray one for another. So here we have all sorts of prayer; ministerial, social, and secret prayer are all recommended. The great advantage and efficacy of prayer are declared and proven. The effectual fervent prayer of a righteous man avails much, whether he prays for himself or others. Note the example of Elijah.

Elias was a man subject to like passions as we are, and he prayed earnestly that it might not rain; and it rained not on the earth by the space of three years and six months. And he prayed again, and the heaven gave rain, and the earth brought forth her fruit.

James 5:17-18

He who prays must be a righteous man; not righteous in an absolute sense (for this Elijah was not, who is here made an example to us), but righteous in a gospel sense, i.e., not loving nor approving of any iniquity. He knew that "*If I regard iniquity in my heart, the Lord will not hear my prayer*" (Psalms 66:18). The prayer itself must be fervent from within.

Note how the prayer must be. It must be a pouring out of the heart to God, and it must proceed from a faith unfeigned. Such prayer avails much. It is of great advantage to ourselves, it may be very beneficial to our friends, and we are assured of it being acceptable to God. It is good having those friends whose prayers are available in the sight of God. The success of Elijah here proves the power of prayer. This may be encouraging to us, even in common cases, if we consider Elijah a man of passion like us. He was a zealous good man and a very great man, but he had his infirmities and was subject to disorder in his passions like others.

In prayer, we must not look to the merit of man but to the grace of God. Only in this, we should copy after Elijah that he prayed earnestly, which was a serious state of mind or as it is in the original, in prayer he prayed. It is not enough to say a prayer; we must pray in prayer. Our thoughts must be fixed on the situation we found in scripture that relates to what we are praying about. Our desires must be firm and passionate in this manner when we pray; we shall speed in prayer and get God's attention more quickly. The Christian's most powerful resource is communion with God through prayer. The results are often greater than one thinks is possible. Many profess to know God and have a close intimate relationship with Him but still see prayer as a last resort after all else fails. We have already discussed

King Saul, who made God a last resort.

The incident of King Saul is in the first Testament, or as most call it, the Old Testament. But I like the first Testament because when something is old, we tend to discard it, failing to see its connection to the second or New Testament. Remember, old and new separate in importance, but first and second join in importance. There is another example of a person making God a last resort in the second or New Testament, and that is the woman with the issue of blood. We always lift the positive about her: she pressed her way through the crowd and touched the hem of His garment, and she was healed. But to every positive, there is a negative. There is a negative side to this woman that we can also learn from: she made God a last resort.

The Scriptures say after she had suffered with the sickness for twelve years, going from doctor to doctor and was not getting better; after she had spent all that she had, she went to Jesus for help. If she hadn't made Jesus a last resort, she would have been healed and wouldn't have been broke.

Both King Saul and the Woman with the Issue of Blood's approaches to God were backward. Prayer should come first. Because God's power is infinitely greater than ours, it only makes sense to rely on it, especially because God encourages us to do so. Elijah prayed that it might not rain, and God heard him in his pleading against an idolatrous persecuting king and people so that it rained not on the earth for the space of three years and six months. Again he prayed, and the heaven gave rain. We can plainly see that prayer is the key that opens and shuts heaven. If Elijah, by prayer, could do such great and wonderful things, surely the prayers of the righteous shall not return void. There may not be much of a miracle in God answering our prayers, yet there may be as much grace as it was with Elijah. Remember now that Elijah was a man of passion, just like you and I. Allow that to register, and we will stop thinking that Elijah had the upper hand on us. God just wants us to have the heart of Elijah; he felt the same as God, and he identified with God. After three and a half years, Elijah prayed for rain, and God answered.

Then he prayed for rain, and down it poured. The grass turned green, and the crops began to grow again.

James 5:18

It is also recorded in the Book of Kings.

I Kings 18:42-45

So Ahab prepared a feast. But Elijah climbed to the top of Mount Carmel and fell to the ground, and prayed. Then he said to his servant, 'Go and look out toward the sea.' The servant went and looked, but he returned to Elijah and said, 'I didn't see anything.' Seven times Elijah told him to go and look, and seven times he went. Finally, in the seventh time, his servant told him, 'I see a little cloud about the size of a hand rising from the sea.' Then Elijah shouted, 'Hurry to Ahab and tell him, "Climb into your chariot and go back home. If you don't hurry, the rain will stop you!" And sure enough, the sky was soon black with clouds. A heavy wind brought a terrific rainstorm, and Ahab left quickly for Jezreel.

Note something about Elijah's faith. He believed from a very small indication that God had answered his prayer though he also had to be persistent because he sent his servant six times, and the servant came back with no indication that God would answer. But he kept believing and expecting, and therefore he received. Sometimes God answers prayer by giving us something better than what we asked for.

II Corinthian 12: 7-10

Even though I have received wonderful revelations from God, but to keep me from getting puffed up, I was given a thorn in my flesh, a messenger from Satan to torment me and keep me from getting proud. Three different times I begged the Lord to take it away. Each time he said, 'My gracious favor is all you need. My power works best in your weakness.' So now I am glad to boast about my weaknesses, so that the power of Christ may work through me. Since I know it is all for Christ's good, I am quite content with my weaknesses and with insults, hardships, persecutions, and calamities. For when I am weak, then I am strong.

Since God loves us, He will hide pride from us and keep us from being exalted above measure. And spiritual burdens are ordered to cure spiritual pride. Paul's thorn in the flesh is said to be a messenger of Satan, which he did not send with a good design, but on the contrary, with ill intentions to discourage the apostle (who had been so highly favored of God) and hinder him in his work. But God designed this for good, and He overruled it and made this messenger of Satan so far from being a hindrance that it was a help to the apostle. The apostle prayed earnestly to God for the removal of this sore grievance.

Note that prayer is a salve for every sore, a remedy for every malady, and when we are afflicted with thorns in the flesh, we ought to give ourselves to prayer. Therefore we are sometimes tempted that we may learn to pray. The apostle besought the Lord thrice that it might depart from him. Afflictions are sent for our spiritual benefit, yet we may pray to God for their removal of them. We ought indeed to desire also that they may reach the end for which they are designed. I have already shared with you in previous chapters that prayer is not just for us to receive from God but for God to get His hands on us. The apostle prayed earnestly and repeated his requests. So if an answer is not given to the first prayer or the second, we must hold on and hold out until we receive an answer. Christ himself prayed to his Father three times.

As troubles are sent to teach us to pray, so they are continued to teach us to continue to be persistent in prayer. Satan can inflict disease. It is written that the LORD said unto Satan, "*Behold, he is in thine hand; but save his life. So went Satan forth from the presence of the LORD, and inflicted Job with sore boils from the sole of his foot unto the crown of his head.*" (Job 2:6-7). Please note that Satan had to seek permission from God to inflict pain upon Job. Know that when God gives permission, He is watching every move that is made against us. God limits Satan; this is why we must stop giving the devil credit for something he is only doing with God's permission. And in this case, He did not allow Satan to destroy. With far too many people, the wrong one gets recognized when we, as children of God, are going through something.

Note that our Lord Jesus Christ prayed three times in Matthew's gospel.

Matthew 26: 39-44

He went on a little farther and fell face down on the ground, praying, 'My Father! If it is possible, let this cup of suffering be taken away from me. Yet I want your will to be done, not mine.' Then he returned to the disciples and found them asleep. He said to Peter, 'Couldn't you stay awake and watch with me even one hour? Keep alert and pray. Otherwise temptation will overpower you. For though the spirit is willing enough, but the body is weak!' Again he left them and prayed, 'My Father! If this cup cannot be taken away until I drink it, your will be done.' He returned to them again and found them sleeping, for they just couldn't keep their eyes open. So he went back to pray a third time, saying the same things again.

He surrendered to God's will. What do you see happening here? What is the principle given here of Jesus praying three times? The more you pray about something, the more assured you become to hang in there and go through it. Jesus was not rebelling against His Father's will when he asked that the cup of suffering and separation be removed. In fact, He reaffirmed His desire to do God's will by saying, "*Yet I want your will, not mine.*" His prayer reveals to us His terrible suffering.

His agony was worse than death because He paid for all sin by being separated from God. The sinless Son of God took our sins upon Himself to save us from suffering and separation. It truly was agony for Jesus because He knew no sin. He had never sinned. It was something pure being infected with a gross germ. It had to be painful, very painful. In times of suffering, people sometimes wish they knew the future, or they wish they could understand the reason for their anguish. Jesus knew what lay ahead for Him, and He knew the reason. Even so, His struggle was intense—more wrenching than any struggle we will ever face. This crisis drove Christ to the most agonizing prayer of His earthly life. Christ going into prayer because of what He was facing is a strong reminder that we should pray.

Prayer is the best practical remedy we can use in times of trouble. Sometimes troubles become so great that prayer seems like the only thing we can do. Prayer is a help that is always near us when we are facing something severe. We are never where we cannot pray. NO crisis, trouble, or trial to test our faith will ever overwhelm us to the point where we cannot pray. Therefore when trouble comes, the first and most important thing to do is pray. The first person we must turn to for help must be our God. We must tell our Father in Heaven all of our sorrows. Although He knows, He waits on us to call upon Him.

Jesus faced one of His greatest crises in the Garden of Gethsemane. The name *Gethsemane* means *oil press*. In regards to what took place in the garden, truly, it was an oil press. Gethsemane was a place where the good olive (Jesus) was crushed by unparalleled agony and yielded the precious oil of His blood so that we could be forgiven, for the scripture says without the shedding of blood, there is no remission of sin. Gethsemane is described in Scripture as a *garden*; however, it was not the average garden of beautiful flowers but a quiet place among the olive trees for Christ to go with His disciples to pray and meditate that night before His crucifixion.

This was not the first time Christ went to Gethsemane. He frequented this place. Luke says that He went, as He was accustomed, to the Mount of Olives. John says that Jesus often resorted there with His disciples. It rejuvenated Him. It is significant that in a garden, Adam's self-indulgence ruined us. Therefore in another garden, the agonies of the Second Adam [Christ] restored us.

The first Adam rebelled in a garden; the second Adam submitted in a garden. In the first garden, it was: my will be done; in the second garden, it was: NOT my will, but thine, be done. In the first garden, sin corrupted. In the second garden, sin was conquered and defeated to where it can no longer reign in our lives. In the first garden, the troubled souls hid from God. In the second garden, the troubled soul earnestly sought God. Christ and the disciples had come from the Upper Room, where they had observed the Passover, and Jesus instituted the Lord's Supper. God answered the Lord's prayer from the garden, but we need to know the sorrow inspiring the prayer. What was it that drove Christ to this most agonizing prayer? What caused Him to face such a great blow suffering so much agony? It was sorrow. His sorrow was "distressful," for He became very heavy. His sorrow was disconcerting or bewildering, for He began to be sore amazed. The phrase *sore amazed* is from one Greek word meaning to throw into terror, to terrify. His sorrow was *disabling*. The idea of disabling means that He was surrounded by grief. He was hemmed in with sorrow, every escape route blocked. Therefore He offered up prayers and supplications with *strong crying and tears*, but He reverently submitted to God.

What are some specifics of the Lord's prayer in the garden? There are some famous pictures of Christ praying in Gethsemane, which have Christ kneeling by some stone, His garments hanging gracefully from His body in perfect order, as He calmly lifts His head in prayer. The pictures portray Jesus as though He is not suffering, but they do not represent Scripture. These pictures remind us that religious artists may not always pay any attention to the details in scripture when they paint their pictures. We need to get our theology from the Word of God, not from some religious painting.

The prayer of Christ was such a solemn prayer that a theologian named S. D. Gordon says that we should approach it with hearts hushed because it was indeed a hallowed event. Matthew says that "He fell on His face," Mark says that "He fell on the ground," and Luke says that "He kneeled." Christ's prayers included all three of the positions. He first kneeled, and then, in the fervency of His prayer and the depth of His sorrow, He fell on the ground, face down. These specifics of Christ's prayer in the Garden give us His "Posture."

Matthew, Mark, and Luke all seem to be giving Christ three different postures in prayer when actually they are only showing the progression that takes place in earnest praying. I know about the progression in posture. One Thursday during my sermon preparation (my members know not to bother me on Thursdays), I was at church alone, just me and the Lord. In my reading and studying, the Spirit of God manifested Himself so strongly in talking with me and revealing what to say in the sermon until I felt so unworthy for Him to come that close to a wretch like me. I began to worship face down in my office and wept.

Christ not only suffered before He prayed; He also suffered while He was praying in such a way that was very afflicting. Luke says that His sweat was, as it were, great drops of blood falling down to the ground. The average person does not understand this. Some want to take this statement as a figure of speech, but the only way one can treat the language right is to take it literally. Christ was experiencing the affliction of a bloody sweat. A "Bloody Sweat!" It troubled me so that I turned to the medical professional in the family and asked my daughter, Dr. Detra Tisdale-Moore, if it were possible for someone to sweat blood. She informed me that it is a very rare condition in which human beings sweat blood called hematohidrosis. It occurs when a person is suffering extreme levels of physical or emotional stress, such as facing one's own death. The severe mental anxiety produces an extreme stress reaction to such a degree that it causes hemorrhage and rupture of blood vessels that supply blood to the sweat glands. This causes the glands to release this vital fluid onto the skin as droplets of blood mixed with sweat. She also pointed out that another effect is that the skin becomes extremely tender and fragile, so any pressure or damage to the skin would be extremely painful.

And that wasn't the only pain that He endured. The greater pain was His separation from His Father. 2 Corinthians 5:21 says He was made "*sin for us.*" Our sins were laid upon Him. Isaiah 53:6 says, "*The Lord hath laid on Him the iniquity of us all.*" To have any sin upon Him was utterly disgusting, nauseating, repulsive, hideous, and gross. We have no idea of what it was like for the infinitely Holy Son of God to take upon Him the awfulness of our iniquities. Not only was He loaded down with guilt, but He was also "*left by God.*" As our substitute, Christ experienced our punishment. It was not just the separation of the soul from the body but the separation of the soul from God.

He cried, "*My God, My God, why hast thou forsaken me?*" The thought of this separation from God was extremely horrific for Christ. Christ only knew close fellowship with God the Father. There had never been any interruption in their fellowship. The fellowship between Father and Son had no beginning or ending until Calvary. The communion of God the Father with God the Son was more blessed than the communion of any others. To have God turn His back on Him was agonizing for the Son of God, who knew nothing else up to that moment; to lose fellowship with His Father meant infinite suffering. What does it take for you to say, "I want your will for my life?" It takes firm trust in God's plans; it takes prayer and obedience each step of the way. We have an account of the answer given to the apostle Paul's prayer regarding the thorn in his flesh that, although the trouble was not removed, an equivalent should be granted. In other words, God will balance your life, and as long as your life is balanced, you can go on for Him.

Please note that the only way your life will become unbalanced is through your thought life, focusing more on the thorn than the equivalent of grace. Your mind becomes the weight. A balance scale will only tilt when you add more weights to one side or the other. *"And he said unto me, 'My grace is sufficient for thee; for my strength is made perfect in weakness."* Although God accepts the prayer of faith, He does not always answer it the way that we think He should. As He sometimes grants in wrath, so He sometimes denies in love. Furthermore, if God does not remove our troubles and temptations but gives us grace sufficient for them, then we have no reason to complain.

We shouldn't complain or say that He is dealing wrongfully toward us. It ought to be of great comfort to us that whatever thorns in the flesh we are panged with, God's grace is sufficient for us. Grace signifies two things: (1) The goodwill of God is towards us.

This should be enough to enlighten us that He cares and will be sufficient strength and comfort to support our souls and cheer up our spirits in all afflictions and distresses. (2) The good work of God in us. The grace that we receive from the fullness that is in Christ, the head of our lives; and from Him, there shall be communicated that which is suitable and seasonable, and sufficient for his members. He will personally talk with you through the situation.

Christ Jesus understands our case and knows our needs, and He will proportion the remedy to our malady, meaning that God will adjust a part or thing in size relative to other parts or things for our good. And then He will not only strengthen us but will also glorify Himself. His strength is made perfect in our weakness. As a result, His grace is manifested and magnified. He ordains His praise out of the mouths of babes and suckling. Perhaps you ask why?

Even everyone that is called by my name: for I have created him for my glory, I have formed him; yea, I have made him.

Isaiah 43:7

Here is the use which the apostle makes of this dispensation: He gloried in his infirmities. Although God did not remove Paul's affliction, He promised to demonstrate His power in Paul. The fact that God's power is displayed in our weaknesses should give us courage and hope.

But God hath chosen the foolish things of the world to confound the wise; and God hath chosen the weak things of the world to confound the things which are mighty; And base things of the world, and things which are despised, hath God chosen, yea, and things which are not, to bring to naught things that are; That no flesh should glory in his presence.

I Corinthians 1:27-29

As we recognize our limitations, we will depend more on God for our effectiveness rather than on our energy, effort, or talent. Our limitations not only help develop Christian character but also deepen our worship because in admitting them, we affirm God's strength. In this, God gets what He wants in allowing us to go through hard times. We often complain about hard times, but I have personally discovered that God is never idle in your life. He is always doing something. He was developing me, making me more like Him. A baby that never moves or struggles in the womb concerns the mother carrying the child. A pearl is formed from a grain of sand or irritant that gets inside an oyster shell and stimulates a defense mechanism that produces a fluid that coats the irritant and produces a pearl. Paul says in Philippians 4:13, "For I can do everything with the help of Christ who gives me the strength I need." Can we really do everything? The power we receive in union with Christ is sufficient to do His will and face the challenges arising from our commitment to doing it. He does not grant us the superhuman ability to accomplish anything we can imagine without regard to His interests. Christ's interest is to make us like unto Himself so we might be with Him. As we contend for the faith, we will face troubles, pressures, and trials. As they come, ask (beg) Christ to strengthen you. Paul took pleasure in suffering.

Therefore I take pleasure in infirmities, in reproaches, in necessities, in persecutions, in distresses for Christ's sake; for when I am weak, then am I strong.

2 Corinthians 12:10

He does not mean sinful infirmities (those we have reason to be ashamed of and grieved over), but he means afflictions, reproaches, necessities, persecutions, and distresses for Christ's sake. The reason for his glory and joy on account of these things was because they were fair opportunities for Christ to manifest the power and sufficiency of His grace resting upon him. When we are strong in abilities or resources, we are tempted to do God's work on our own, which can lead to pride. When we are weak, allowing God to fill us with His power, we are stronger than we could ever be on our own.

I understand now why the church that I am currently pastoring is named Rehoboth; it means so much to God. Let me share with you why. Rehoboth is a church that was brought into existence from much agonizing prayer from both pastor and the people.

The former church that I pastored had gone through an unpleasant experience. I was told to go against my biblical conviction concerning women preachers. I couldn't find in scripture where Jesus Christ, the head of the church, called a woman to that high position, going against the order of His Father, who put her in subjection to man. Jesus says in John 10:30, "I and my Father are one." He also says in Mark 3:25, "And if a house be divided against itself, that house cannot stand."

But he, knowing their thoughts, said unto them, every kingdom divided against itself is brought to desolation; and a house divided against a house falleth.

Luke 11:17

His calling her to preach would have said that He and His Father were divided. According to the scriptures, when Jesus called His disciples, He prayed all night.

And it came to pass in those days, that He went out into a mountain to pray, and continued all night in prayer to God. And when it was day, He called unto him His disciples; and of them He chose twelve, whom also He named apostles.

Luke 6:12-13

Jesus had some faithful women that were followers of Him, and after praying all night to His Father as to whom He was to select as His disciples, He called all men and sent them forth to preach.

And he goeth up into a mountain, and calleth unto him whom he would: and they came unto him. And he ordained twelve, that they should be with him, and that he might send them forth to preach.

Mark 3:13-14

After I resigned from my pastorate, the people went for choir rehearsal and prayer that Tuesday night following my resignation. They could not get in for prayer. All of the locks on the doors had been changed. When they asked why, they were told that no one was getting back into the church until they cooled off. Therefore they made arrangements with the late Rev. Kimmie Davis, who, at that time, was the pastor of Hope Christian Center located at 405 East College Street in Jackson, Tennessee, and asked if they could have a prayer vigil that Saturday morning, March 4, 1995. That whole process created intense praying for me.

The Lord had told me to resign as a pastor if they didn't accept my conviction concerning women preachers, and I did. But that Sunday morning, the fourth Sunday in February 1995, the late Rev. Joseph Mann, an associate minister at that time, asked for remarks. In his remarks, he polled the congregation, asking how many wanted me to stay as pastor. Two-thirds of the congregation stood and walked forth for me to stay with them. It all began to make sense because the Holy Spirit came to me that week in my office, telling me to make no decision. I was confused because the decision had already been made, for God had told me to resign if they did not accept my conviction, and I had obeyed in resigning as pastor.

After Rev. Mann did what he did, Mrs. Delores Jones asked the chairman of deacons and the chairman of trustees, "What are you going to do, for as you can see, the church has spoken." I came back to the pulpit and told all of them who stood forth for me to stay with them, "I see what you are saying, and I hear what you are saying, but the Lord has directed me to make no decision." The Lord moved upon the congregation that Sunday morning, knowing that I wouldn't walk away from that many people who wanted me to stay without coming back to Him for directions. The Holy Spirit led me to check into a hotel with no one knowing where I was, not even my wife. I checked into Budgetel Inn, room 109 (currently La Quinta Inn). I was locked up with God all night and wrestled with Him in prayer like Jacob did with the angel at Peniel in Genesis 32:24-25.

The Spirit led me to take three books to the hotel room with me—my Bible, a concordance, and a book entitled, *Preaching Through a Storm* by Dr. H. Beecher Hick, Jr. I had heard the name Rehoboth before from the late Rev. Dr. Alfred Dewayne Hill of Memphis, Tennessee who conducted a revival for me when I was the pastor of Oak Hill Baptist Church in Bolivar, Tennessee back in 1983. Dr. Hill preached from Genesis 26:22 the entire week.

The name Rehoboth flashed across my mind because I remembered the name, but I couldn't find it. Evidently, that was the purpose of the concordance because I used it to find the name. I just opened the book that He told me to take with me. The Holy Spirit led me to Chapter 8, page 129 of the book, *Preaching Through a Storm*, where it is written:

"How the church responds to the crisis in its midst will be more important to its continuing life in the long run than who the winners or losers were. Viewed that way, church conflict can have a positive value. We can see it as a learning experience for both the pulpit and pew, and we can seek to gain insight that may help the church face future crises. At some time or another, every preacher comes to the moment when his kingdom is weighed in the balance, and he stands in the tenuous twilight of decision, wondering if he or his ministry will be found seriously wanting."

He further said,

"The first lesson I learned was don't give up the ship, that one is not so much made the pastor as one goes through a long and often frustrating process of becoming the pastor."

At that point, the Lord told me to stay in Jackson and lead the church He was establishing. I did a lot of liquid praying that night, for I wept bitterly, but He would not let me go. Then in chapter 8, page 129 again:

> *"Additionally, the preacher/pastor must come to realize that he is not alone in the boat. There are other passengers who depend upon his steady hand at the helm, and the primary objective of the pilot is not to lose the ship but to land it in the harbor of salvation and safety."*

That Saturday morning, March 4, 1995, I went to the prayer vigil where twenty people from the former church had assembled and were praying and asking God what they would do. I arrived when the prayer vigil was about to dismiss and shared with them what God had revealed to me.

The people rejoiced that day and had their first worship service as a new church on the 1st Sunday in March, March 5, 1995, at 8:00 a.m. in Hope Christian Activity Center 21 years ago. Their prayers were answered, and He has answered many, many more since then. What an experience I had with God as I was a part of Him creating a church for Himself, having it understood from the beginning that she is a *theocracy* and not a *democracy*. A democracy is of the people, by the people, and for the people, whereas a theocracy is just the opposite; it is of God, by God, and for God.

To secure the fact that the church would be governed as a theocracy, The Altar of Seven Bibles was set up the night of the first business meeting to signify how the church would be governed. She would be governed by the Word of God. I remember distinctly hearing His voice telling me to ask seven members to bring me their Bibles. He had me stack them on top of each other on a table, have all the people get on their knees on a cold concrete floor, and commit, entering into a covenant with God that the church with be governed as a theocracy.

After we finished praying, the Lord had me ask for seven Bibles to be encased and placed beside the pulpit. One member, Carlene Spears, raised her hand and said she had just bought three. She brought them up, and another member, Gerald Vann, gave forty dollars to buy the other four. God did not intend us to be weak, passive, or ineffective. Life provides enough hindrances and setbacks without us creating them. When those obstacles come, we must depend on God. Only His power will make us effective for Him and help us do work that has lasting value. Paul had so much experience of the strength of divine grace that he could say, "When I am weak, then am I strong." This is a Christian paradox: when we are weak in ourselves, then we are strong in the grace of our Lord Jesus Christ. When we see ourselves as weak, we go out of ourselves to Christ, and are qualified to receive strength from Him and experience most of the supplies of divine strength and grace. I close this topic, "Does God Always Answer Prayer," with a promise from God.

The eyes of the Lord watch over those who do right, and His ears are open to their prayers. But the Lord turns his face against those who do evil.

I Peter 3:12

PRAYER MUST BE ACCOMPANIED BY A WILLINGNESS TO OBEY

The Lord first led me to experience the need for prayer accompanied by a willingness to obey when I went full-time as a pastor. I became pastor of the Oak Hill Baptist Church in January 1980. I was led to go full-time on June 5, 1986, but the church chose not to support me financially as a full-time pastor. I continued to serve full-time until the fourth Sunday in September 1988. Because of my financial struggles, I was led to resign as pastor, giving them a 90-day notice that went into effect the first Sunday in July 1988.

My whole family was praying. The children had been taught about prayer through their mother having devotion with them every day. During my last 30 days at the Oak Hill Baptist Church, there was much agonizing in prayer to God. I had sent out resumes all over. I was given opportunities to preach at various churches. I had left some churches confident that I would be elected, only to be disappointed. A church in Jackson, Tennessee, Walnut Grove Baptist Church, knew me and my family well. Some of the mothers of the church had helped my wife with the children, and we were well-loved by them and their pastor, the late Rev. S. P. Sanders. Rev. Sanders. He helped us a lot by giving us food, allowing me to preach, and taking up special offerings for me and my family. When he went overseas for 30 days, he left me in charge of the church. It was a great experience for me, and the church was very good to us.

When Pastor Sanders passed on to glory, Walnut Grove needed a pastor. I sent a resume to them, and they were glad to receive it. I was called in for an interview with the pulpit committee and to do my first sermon. The interview went well, and they enjoyed the sermon, but I heard the voice of the Lord say to me, "This is not where I'm sending you." This led me to pray even harder.

I was interviewing with the Cumberland Baptist Church in Jackson, Tennessee when Walnut Grove called me in to preach my second trial sermon leading up to the 4th Sunday in September, my last Sunday at Oak Hill Baptist Church. My 90 days were almost up, and I was confident that Walnut Grove would elect me. After the second sermon, I was called in for another meeting with the pulpit committee. When I walked into the church for the second meeting, the Lord's voice changed, and it was heavier and stronger, saying,

"I told you; this is not where I'm sending you." Walnut Grove was electing that Friday night leading up to the 4th Sunday in September, and Cumberland Baptist Church was electing that Monday night after the 4th Sunday in September. I felt that He was sending me to Cumberland, but they weren't going to elect until that Monday night, and I was getting ready to receive my last check on that 4th Sunday morning. After that, I didn't know where my next red cent would come from. How was I going to provide for my family? This is when I learned that the saying "a bird in the hand is worth two in the bush" doesn't work with God.

All day that Friday, I agonized with God in prayer over what to do. I had a family of five to provide for, and all He would say to me was, "I'm not sending you to Walnut Grove." Walnut Grove was to meet at 6 P.M. that Friday to elect a pastor. I sat my wife down and told her we wouldn't have an income after Sunday and that Walnut Grove would elect in about an hour. I admitted to her that I strongly felt they would elect me, but the Lord had told me He was not sending me to them. I asked her what I should do. "That is between you and the Lord," she replied.

I picked up the phone and called Ms. Willie Mae Summers, who was on the pulpit committee for Walnut Grove, and told her to remove me as a candidate. She asked me why and said that she was sure I would be elected. I informed her that the Lord was not sending me to them.

As my family and I walked across the parking lot on my last Sunday at Oak Hill, my youngest daughter, Detra (who was thirteen then), said, "Daddy, don't worry. If He feeds the birds of the air, He will take care of us." Sure enough, that following Monday night, Cumberland Baptist Church elected me as their pastor with double my previous salary, a parsonage, and full benefits. Isn't God awesome?

The Bible is filled with examples to show that there must be a willingness to obey God before He can bless you.

Then the Lord said to Moses, 'Why are you crying out to me? Tell the people to get moving!

Exodus 14:15

The Lord told Moses to stop praying and get moving! What was God's reason for saying that to Moses? He expected Moses to trust Him based on what he had already seen and witnessed. Moses was not reflecting on what God had already done, and this is what we fail to do so many times. Prayer always has a vital place in our lives, but there is also a time and a place for action. Sometimes we know what to do, but we pray for more guidance as an excuse to postpone doing what we need to do. If we know what to do, it is time to get moving. We have here direction given to Israel's leader. What must he do himself? He must, for the present, leave off praying and apply himself to the business at hand.

God said to him, "Wherefore cry thou unto me?" Moses had been brought to the point where he needed to reflect on what God had already done and then trust and obey when he couldn't see any way out of what seemed inevitable. I believe that Moses didn't cry to God audibly anymore, but I'm confident that as he moved out, he kept lifting his heart to God in meditational prayer. Moses' silent prayers of faith prevailed more with God than Israel's loud outcries of fear. Note that praying with the right heart posture is crying to God. It is the language of both a natural and an importunate desire that is urgent and consists of being overly persistent in your request. I have come to understand through my experience in life that obedience doesn't just happen all of a sudden as if you just up and obey the directives of God. There has to be a willingness to trust, which has to be built through spending time with God and keeping company with Him throughout the day.

Watch ye therefore, and pray always, that ye may be accounted worthy to escape all these things that shall come to pass, and to stand before the Son of man.

Luke 21:36

We are to.....

Rejoice in hope; have patience in tribulation; continuing instant in prayer.

Romans 12:12

Pray in the Spirit at all times in every prayer and supplication. To that end, keep alert and always persevere in supplication for all the saints.

Ephesians 6:18

Devote yourselves to prayer, keeping alert in it with thanksgiving. We are to pray without ceasing

Colossians 4:2

In everything give thanks for it is the will of God in Christ Jesus concerning you.

I Thessalonians 5:18

Moses had something else to do besides praying; he was to command the hosts of Israel, and it was now necessary that he should be at his post. The people were looking to him, and that required compulsory, indispensable praying, with which I became very acquainted when Rehoboth was established. What was Moses to order Israel to do? Speak to them so that they go forward. Some think that Moses had prayed, but not so much for their deliverance (he was assured of that). He prayed for the pardon of their murmuring and that God's ordering them to go forward indicated the pardon. There is no going forward with any comfort but in the sense of our reconciliation to God.

Moses had bidden them to stand still and expect orders from God, and now orders were given. They thought they must have been directed either to the right hand or to the left. "No," says God, "speak to them to go forward," directly into the sea as if a fleet of transport ships had been ready for them to embark in. Note that when you are in the way of your duty, though you are met with difficulties, you must go forward and not stand in mute astonishment; you must be mindful of the present work and then leave the event to God. Use the means available to you and trust Him with the matter.

After Rehoboth was established and had her first worship service, I had an experience similar to Moses'. I knew they would need a place of worship, a home, so I started praying and looking. My prayers were accompanied by my willingness to move out. I went looking, and I also had other members of the church praying as well.

When I learned of a building on Campbell extended or Old Humboldt Road that a family used for worship, I had to start praying as I worked. Therefore I went to look at the building, but the Lord didn't give me peace of mind over the building.

We kept praying, and after about four months, I was told about a Presbyterian church on Hollywood Avenue that would be sold. The building didn't have a baptistery, but there was a place for one. It had a fully equipped daycare center, and one of the members of Rehoboth was qualified to run it. They were asking $85,000.00 for the church. I went and looked at it, and it was ideal. So I proceeded to claim it through prayer. I walked around it in broad daylight once a day for six days, and on the seventh day, I did it seven times as God had Joshua command the armed soldiers to march around the wall of Jericho, and then I claimed it. Although God was leading me, I was influenced by how I'd had to lead in the past, and I gathered some members together and brought them over to see the church that God had provided for us through following God's directives. You will later see that this involvement was a costly mistake because this was not what God had intended for me to do.

I was put in touch with the pastor of another Presbyterian church on North Highland Avenue, overseeing this facility's sale. The pastor met with me about the church. He sent me, and I took one of the church's members, the late Bro. Ernest Mitchell (the treasurer) to Memphis to the headquarters of the Presbyterian Church. We met with the leader, and he confirmed that they would sell. I told him that the Lord had established a church and we needed a home. He was glad Rehoboth was established and prayed with us in his office. We returned to Jackson believing the Lord would give us this church. This is how I know that prayer has to be coupled with obedience. If you don't obey against the odds, you won't get your answer to prayer.

The Lord sent me to Union Planters Bank, and I asked for a meeting with the president I had never met. His name was Mr. Gary Grisham. I walked in without an appointment and asked for him. His secretary informed him I was there, and he came out of his office and asked how he could help me. I extended my hand, and we gave each other a firm handshake. I told him who I was and then said, "The Lord sent me to you for you to buy us a church." I could see the puzzled look on his face, but he took me to his office and asked me to tell him what I was talking about. I shared with him what God was doing. I told him about my one-room hotel experience in room 109, where I wrestled with God all night, trying to get out of what He commanded me to do: lead a church that He was establishing. Mr. Grisham listened to the whole story and was moved by God to hear the story again the following week, only this time with his Vice President, Mr. Ben Rudd. After I told the identical story again, Mr. Grisham's exact words to his vice president were, "This man will work with you from now on."

The next week, I met again with the members I had shown the church building, but they did not understand how God was leading me. I did not fully understand how God was leading me. I learned later that I was not supposed to have second-guessed God by assembling some people and telling them what He was doing with me, but I was so used to working that way. In talking with them, I was encouraged not to give them the full asking price of $85,000 but to negotiate and get them to come down when the Lord had already given it to us. I listened to the people, and we are suffering the consequences to this day.

It was later made known that another church

established longer than Rehoboth was also interested in the building. One of the prominent members of the Presbyterian church that was on the committee to sell this facility had promised the church to the pastor of another Church, and she was working hard for him to get it. Another member of the committee that we were put in touch with through the headquarters in Memphis was working with me for the sale of the church. I presented a negotiated price, which was turned down, stating they had to have $85,000. My committee person had me make my offer, and he would turn it in. It was $65,000, and they denied it. I followed up with the committee members, and this time I told them we would submit the full price. When I told the sales committee person working with me that we would give what they were asking, the other sales committee member told the pastor of the other church to offer $85,100. It was a very unfortunate mistake for us not to offer them the full price upfront. Therefore, we were outbid by a very small margin of $100. Disappointed and somewhat discouraged, I had to draw upon the fact that Rehoboth was established by God. I knew it was not my doing, and God told me in room 109, "I'll be with you." Therefore, I encouraged myself and the members to claim that the Lord would give us a home.

About a month later, another opportunity became available. Pastor Dennis Blalock of New St. Luke Baptist Church was a friend to Pastor Charlie Caruthers, the pastor of the True Believers Holiness Church. Pastor

Caruthers was then renting the Nazarene church that the Lord would provide for us. He told Pastor Blalock that the Nazarene church wanted to sell the building, and he didn't think they would buy it. Pastor Blalock then told me to check into it. I was put in touch with Pastor Caruthers, who had me contact the late Mr. Don Holdaway. Mr. Holdaway was determined that we would get the church, as the Lord would also have it, because a developer was building some condominiums behind the church, and they would have bought it had they known that it was for sale. The Nazarene church wanted well over twice as much as the other church. I went to Union Planters Bank and gave them the price. They agreed to loan us 80% of the appraisal price, but they would need some collateral. Seven members were willing to put up their property for collateral. Their property was appraised, and the amounts were put in sealed envelopes. I took them to the bank and gave them to the loan officer, Mr. Ben Rudd. I was thankful, but God didn't want anybody to be able to say that if it hadn't been for them putting up their property, we wouldn't have this church building.

The week before the closing of the loan, I went by to see if everything was ready for the closing. Mr. Rudd reached into his desk drawer and gave me the letters back unopened. "We don't need these," he stated. So I gave them all back to the members sealed, just like they were given to me. Then, about a year later, Mr. Rudd and I talked about the purchase of the church, and he asked, "What did you put up for collateral?"

I replied, "Nothing. I brought seven sealed envelopes from members who had their property appraised, but you didn't use them; you gave them back to me." He didn't remember giving the letters back to me.

Then, a few more years later, I went to see another loan officer at another branch about some personal business, and he asked about the purchase of the church on Wallace Road. He asked, "What did you put up for collateral when you purchased that church?"

"Nothing," I replied.

"Nothing?" he questioned. I explained that I had brought collateral to be used, but they didn't use it when we got ready to close the loan. He told me that he didn't see how a loan of that amount was approved. He said a loan that size would have had to go through corporate in Nashville, Tennessee, and they would not have approved it without collateral. He was shocked.

Rehoboth still needed to come up with the other 20%. It looked dim, but God came through again! Mr. Don Holdaway told Bro. Mitchell and me that their headquarters was in Nashville, TN. He told us to go and talk with the president of the Nazarene Churches in Tennessee about whether they would finance that 20%. Bro. Earnest Mitchell Jr. encouraged me to visit Nashville to see if they would finance the 20%. My wife and I had to go to Atlanta, GA, to see our daughter, who was attending Spelman College at that time. I made an appointment with Rev. Johnson, the

President of the Nazarene churches. We explained to him the situation of the church. The Lord worked for Rehoboth that day! Rev. Johnson agreed to finance the other 20%. He prayed and rejoiced with my wife and me in his office. Upon receiving the good news, I called Bro. Earnest Mitchell Jr. He rejoiced and called Sis. Delores Jones and informed her and other members that God had made a way.

On the 1st Sunday in June 1996, a new day dawned for Rehoboth Baptist Church. God had made room for us! We had prayed and worked long hours with the hope and expectation that Rehoboth would one day realize her full potential in doing what the Lord would have all His churches to do, evangelizing and making disciples, and receiving the ministry of reconciliation with joy. The week before the march to our new home, Bro Earnest Mitchell Jr. and I worked hard to prepare the building for the first worship service. There was a lot to be done. Many of the pews for the sanctuary were unassembled and scattered all over the building. A big enclosure for their PA system was in the sanctuary and had to be torn out and pews put in its place. No pews were assembled in the choir stand at all. Mr. Holdaway had built a wall behind the pulpit chairs separating the choir from the pulpit area. That Saturday, many members came over and gave the Lord's house, our new home, a thorough cleaning for the first worship service.

The forecast said it was to rain that Saturday night

before the march, and it did. It was a downpour even though the people and I prayed for God to hold the rain. On June 2, 1996, at 6:30 A.M., the Rehoboth Baptist Church Family gathered at the Hope Christian Center parking lot at 405 E. College Street to march to the new home God had given us. It was still raining heavily on that Sunday morning when we prepared for the 5-mile march. The escort from the Jackson Police Department arrived at the church and asked me what we would do. We decided that we would march despite the rain. I assembled the people in the rain and told them to remember what the Lord has done for them on this day. With umbrellas and raincoats, the late Rev. Joseph Mann and I started carrying the Altar of Seven Bibles, followed by the men of the church who rotated out carrying the Altar with all of the members who came down for the march. The journey began.

One member, Sis. Juanita Marshall, whose ankles would swell if she walked a long way, decided to walk for God despite the risk of being unable to go to work the next day because of swollen ankles. Her ankles did not swell. Some of the members who were up in age, including one of the mothers of the church, the late Sis. Eula Mae Joyner (then 88 years old), rode the church van. Another mother, the late Sis. Lottie White (who was in her mid 60's then) walked the distance, and several members followed in their cars. We sang and praised God as we walked.

After the first mile, the rain began to subside. We

continued marching and singing. The Altar continued to be alternately carried by the men of the church. The late Rev. Charles Rainer, the pastor of Pilgrim Rest Baptist Church and a dear friend, marched with us. Bro. Roy Hill video-taped the historical event. Friends, family, and well-wishers marched at different locations along our route. As we marched past homes, people stood at their doors in amazement. Others waved and smiled. Approximately 1 mile from our new home, the rain stopped, the sun appeared, and the congregation shouted! We could see our new home, and I told the members, "Rehoboth, Canaan is up ahead!" The members who went to the building to prepare for the arrival of those who marched that morning heard us coming. They came onto the lawn and cheered as we approached our new home.

Upon our arrival at our new home at 810 Wallace Road, I had everyone come out and assemble behind me and Rev. Mann. Everyone was led into the church by the Altar of Seven Bibles. We entered the building, singing and praising God for His mighty work! The Altar was placed in its permanent home, where it still stands to this day next to the pulpit. Everyone was assembled around the altar for prayer to thank God for His blessings. I prayed to God that if any member came before this Altar and prayed that God was to hear from heaven and answer them. Then we began our first worship service in our new home. The first sermon was entitled "Tragedy or Triumph." No text was given. It was from the book *Preaching through a Storm* by H. Beecher Hicks, Jr., one of the three books the Holy Spirit had me take to the hotel.

The day was filled with praises and fellowship. A feast was prepared and held unto God according to Exodus 5:1. There was rejoicing, praising, and giving God all glory. He had made room for us!

Another experience that the Lord carried me through in 2010 relates to the need for our prayers to be accompanied by a willingness to obey. The church home, the place of worship the Lord blessed us to acquire in 1996, needed repairs. The building had two extended flat roofs on both sides that were leaking badly. We started having problems with the flat roofs around 1998. We brought roofers that applied different layers of covering material to stop the leaks. That worked for a while, but the leaks would start back. After being in the building for 14 years, there was deterioration from the leaks involving both the exterior and interior of the building. Despite the church's and various members' efforts to fix up the church and make the Lord's house look good, it still needed a lot more work.

The late Rev. Joseph Mann had a son who lived in another city named John Mann, who was an architect. He agreed to draw the plans for the renovation. I had the plan encased and mounted in the hallway of the church. I asked the members to make a financial pledge, and many of the members did. My wife and I pledged $1,000.00. In 2010, it was time to refinance the loan. The country was in a recession, making it very difficult to borrow money. I returned to the same bank that bought the church building, and Mr. Gary Grisham was still the president. He contacted our loan officer, Mr. Bryce West, vice president of the Greystone branch out north. He told him what we wanted to do. Mr. Grisham and Mr. West were concerned about increasing the loan because we were in a recession. They knew it was time to refinance the loan, and it would have been alright with the bank to refinance it without adding anything to the loan. They came by the church office to see me, and I shared with them the condition of the church, that it badly needed some repairs, and we wanted to renovate to move the bathrooms close to the sanctuary. They didn't have vents, and sometimes the bathroom odor would drift into the sanctuary. We wanted to move them and put classrooms on that side of the building.

I made several trips to Mr. Grisham and Mr. West's office, delivering financial reports of the church income, showing that we could handle the increase. We kept praying for the loan. I had said to Mr. Grisham that we had some strong tithers, that we would be alright, then a test came from the Lord as to where our trust was, in Him or tithing members.

While negotiating the loan, one of the church's biggest tithers got upset with me and left the church. That was a devastating blow to the church's income. Somehow, Mr. Grisham learned of it and confronted me. He caught me off guard, but God was right there. I didn't become nervous because the Holy Spirit kept me calm. I experienced what the scripture says about being before the magistrates.

And when they bring you unto the synagogues, and unto magistrates, and powers, take ye no thought how or what thing ye shall answer, or what ye shall say: For the Holy Ghost shall teach you in the same hour what ye ought to say.

Luke 12:11-12

I calmly said, "Mr. Grisham, I was wrong to tell you that God would have us trust in anybody but Him."

On their second trip to my office, I had the church treasurer there, Bro Keith Gibson, in the meeting with us. He missed a lot of meetings because he drove a truck, but he was at this one. When Mr. Grisham finished laying out everything, Bro. Keith said, "I don't know, pastor."

Mr. Grisham immediately told me, "It looks like you and your treasurer are not together.

I said, "Oh no, we are together. He hasn't had time to review the church's financial records, but he is with me." When He and Mr. West made the third trip to my office at Rehoboth, I told him that Bro. Keith had looked at the records and was on board. I never will forget this. As a matter of fact, I really appreciated his using scripture because it said to me that he was a man of the Word. Mr. Grisham was a Christian and a praying man; he came with scripture to support their skepticism about increasing the loan.

For which of you, intending to build a tower, sitteth not down first, and counteth the cost, whether he have sufficient to finish it?

Luke 14:28

Again, the Lord kept me calm. I told him, "You are putting scripture on me, I really appreciate that, but we have counted the cost." And thank God we haven't missed a payment. Therefore in refinancing the loan, we borrowed enough to do an extensive renovation of the church, from the inside and out. We added on to the existing building, plus the inside of the current building was gutted, and we came back with new Sunday school classrooms, an associate ministers' office, a completely refurbished sanctuary, and a new pastor's office that included a library, lounge area, and bathroom.

This is where much prayer had to be accompanied by a willingness to obey. About halfway through the construction, while everything was all torn up, the city engineer came over to inspect the work being done. The job supervisor had already been on the roof and saw how bad the flat roofs were. He told me later that he didn't want the inspector to go up there because he knew what was going to happen, and sure enough, he went up on the roof and saw how bad they were from the layers of material that had been stacked on top of each other to stop the leaks. The heat from the sun and heavy snows from the previous winters had caused it to buckle, and it became very lumpy and warped. The city engineer told us that we had to replace them.

I got a quote for how much it would cost to fix the flat roofs. One person told me around $50,000. We had already borrowed all we could and didn't have another $50,000. Brasfield Construction Company, the contractor of the job, told us about a person they worked with that did roofs, and he gave us a price of around $35,000, which was much better than $50,000.

The engineer shut down the construction, telling us that we had to fix those flat roofs or we couldn't go any further on the old construction. They would only be able to continue working on the new addition. I was not only the pastor; I was also the job supervisor. And not only was I supervising what was going on at church, but my personal home was also being renovated at the same time. I went into prayer. That was all I could do, and that was all I knew to do. I remembered the Lord working with me in room 109, telling me what to do when the church was established. I needed Him again to tell me what to do, so I returned to the same hotel and asked for room 109, but it was occupied, so they gave me room 103. I checked in and did the same thing I had done in room 109. I just turned the little light on over the desk in the room. There was continual agonizing with God in prayer. I prayed until I got sleepy.

While praying, the Lord told me to turn it in to the insurance company. I went to bed, and He put me to sleep. While asleep, I had a dream of the hotel being on fire. People were scrambling down the hallway screaming, "Get out! Get out! The building is on fire!" I was trying to wake up and couldn't. When I awoke, I heard a voice say, "It's over now." I didn't know what the dream was all about. I called the insurance company the next day, and they sent a claims adjuster out. He went up to the top of the building and saw the condition of those flat roofs. He told me that he would turn in his report, but he didn't think they would be able to help us. I wouldn't accept that because I knew the Lord had told me to turn it in to the insurance company. Therefore, I kept praying and calling them until they finally sent an engineer.

He went up to the top of the roof and turned in his report. They followed up with me and said they couldn't help us because the damage was not their fault and was not covered under the policy.

There was a local adjuster that Brasfield Construction knew. They called him, and I let him look over our policy. He told me that the insurance company had us, and nothing in the policy indicated that they had to help. At that point, I was stressed out. I represent a legal service known then as Pre-Paid Legal Services (now known as Legal Shield, and I still have the service). I called them to see if they could help. I told them my situation, and they had me fax the policy to them. They examined the policy and discovered that the policy stated that if there was heavy snow during the times of the leaks, they had to help us. And sure enough, we'd had a heavy snow. I told the legal service that others had looked at the policy, and no one else had found what they did. They told me that they write policies and know and understand the language. Thank God for Legal Shield! We couldn't afford an attorney, but the law firm represented the church because I was the pastor and had the service. Now churches have to have their own policy, and the way they fought for me, I would encourage them to get this service.

I informed the adjusters of what our attorney had found in the policy, and the insurance company was still being stubborn. The legal service wrote letters and talked to the adjusters. The insurance company knew they had to do something, but they were delaying it as long as possible, and time was running out. I kept agonizing with God in prayer until one day, God encouraged me to keep fighting. He had Rev. Travis Brown, one of the associate ministers of the church who was then pastoring the St. Paul Baptist Church in Milan, Tennessee, come to see me. When he got to the church, I wasn't there, so he just sat in his car in the heat of the day, waiting on me to come (and it was very hot that day). When I finally arrived at the church, I went out and sat in the car with him, and since he was an associate minister of the church, I started telling him everything I was going through. He just sat and listened. Then I told him about the dream that I had in the hotel room. He told me that God had given him the gift of interpreting dreams, and he interpreted my dream for me. He said that the dream was indicating that the insurance company was going to fight me, but I was going to win. After talking with him, the Lord directed me to go higher in the insurance company, and I obeyed. I went to the top, to the head of the claims division. I got his number through customer service, and I called him. I told him what my problem was. He told me that he would pull my file and look at it.

About three days passed, and I didn't hear from him, so I called him back and prayed while on hold. He finally came to the phone and told me that he reviewed my file and said that it looked like, and then there was pause... and he said, "Maybe we were a little hard on you. We are going to give you $20,000." And that was all that we needed. We had the rest. I believe he was getting ready to say "no" like the rest, but God turned his heart, which was why he paused. I had been praying God's Word back to Him.

The king's heart is in the hand of the Lord; as the rivers of waters, He turneth it whithersoever He will. "

Proverbs 21:1

The word "king's" in the original Hebrew language can be understood as being anyone in authority. Therefore, I can tell you from experience that prayer must be accompanied by a willingness to obey.

PRAYING IN THE NAME OF JESUS

The Bible states in John 14:14, "If ye shall ask anything in my name, I will do it." What a broad promise! Anything? Does this mean that, whether large or small, all our needs are covered by the word *anything*? Just reading this from the Bible without proper understanding, a person could see the use of Jesus' name as a magic wand, but that is not what Jesus is giving us. As a matter of fact, this promise is not given to the general public but to a specific group, the twelve disciples who had given up all to follow Him. They had spent three-and-a-half years with Him. They understood the requirement that went along with such a declaration.

When reading the Bible, we must keep scripture in context, applying the five "W's" of interpretation:

- *Who* wrote it?
- *What* was going on when it was written?
- *When* was it written?

- *Where* was it written?
- *Why* was it written?

In this scripture, John, the beloved disciple, is the author. Jesus was training the twelve disciples (*what*) at the close of his ministry on Earth (*when*). The scene is in Galilee (*where*). Jesus was preparing to return to the Father in heaven (*why*) and wanted to ensure the disciples were ready for life after his ascension. Therefore giving an extensive promise like that to the twelve meant that He knew they would ask for things pertaining to the kingdom as they had been trained. Read the context:

Verily, verily, I say unto you, He that believeth on me, the works that I do shall he do also; and greater works than these shall he do; because I go unto my Father. And whatsoever ye shall ask in my name, that will I do, that the Father may be glorified in the Son. If ye shall ask any thing in my name, I will do it.

John 14:12-14

If you have a good study Bible, verse 15 presents another thought. This promise only works for dedicated disciples. Praying in Jesus' name means praying in Jesus' character because, from a biblical perspective, a name depicts character. We are always to ask "in" the name of Jesus and not just "with" the name of Jesus. "With" is an attempt to use Him, but "In" means that you know Him personally. While the proper use of His name encourages us and honors Him, it also puts a requirement upon us.

I dare not use my Lord's name for a selfish or willful petition. I may only use my Lord's name for prayers He would pray if He were in my situation. It is a high privilege to be authorized to ask in the name of Jesus as if Jesus Himself asked, but our love for Him will never allow us to set that name where He would not. When I use His name, I must ask for what Jesus approves. Then I have that which I seek of the Father. Dare I put His seal to my prayer if it's all about me and my concerns and not His? There is much to understand about the use of Jesus' name. Many names are dear, but the dearest one, which grows dearer with time, is the simple but sublime name of "Jesus." Paul had such a profound respect for it that he called it "the name that is above every name" (Philippians 2:9). When we come to the last judgment, even those condemned will recognize Jesus' authority and right to rule. People can choose now to commit their lives to Jesus as Lord because, in the end, they will be forced to acknowledge Him as Lord. Christ may return at any moment. Are you prepared to meet Him?

Jesus was raised from the dead; Christ is now the head of the church, the ultimate authority over the world. Jesus is the Messiah, God's anointed one, the one Israel longed for, but He has already come, the one they looked for who will set their broken world right. As disciples, we can be confident that God has won the final victory and controls everything. We need not fear any dictator, nation, or even death or Satan himself. The contract has been signed and sealed; we are waiting just a short while for delivery.

Jesus is the name the angel announced before Christ was born and represented Him as a gift from heaven, which in his person would fulfill the promise of Jehovah to save His people. "J-E-S-U-S," The "JE" is the first syllable—Je, Jeho, or Jah. Jehovah – this name of God speaks of divine authority that Jesus came as the great "I AM." The syllable tells us of His eternal Godhead, covenant relations, mighty power, and love. All the virtues seen in the Jehovah of old manifested in Him who came from heaven. The next syllable, "SUS," is associated with the name Oshea, Hosea, or Houshaia, meaning "Help," which was the name of the spies sent out by Moses. But He changed it to Jehoshua, signifying Jehovah our Savior or deliverer, or the help of Jehovah. Jesus is the Greek form of Joshua. Therefore in the second part of Jesus' name, we are assured of pardon and peace, of deliverance from sin and hell. The name of Jesus means the salvation of God or God the Savior. The matchless name of Jesus, therefore, expresses the relation of Jehovah to him in incarnation by which he humbled himself and became obedient unto death, even the death of the cross. In the progressive revelation of prayer, Christ declared the necessity of presenting our petitions in His name and the Father's name. To whom exactly are we to pray? According to scripture, we are to pray to God the Father, who hears and answers prayer.

But when you pray, go away by yourself, shut the door behind you, and pray to your Father secretly. Then your Father, who knows all secrets, will reward you.

Matthew 6:6

We are to pray to God the Son as one who is coequal with the Father. Note the prayer of Stephen in the book of Acts:

And as they stoned him, Stephen prayed, 'Lord Jesus, receive my spirit.' And he fell to his knees, shouting, 'Lord, don't charge them with this sin!' And with that, he died.

Acts 7:59-60

He prayed to Jesus. As Stephen died, he spoke words very similar to Jesus' words on the cross.

Then said Jesus, 'Father, forgive them; for they know not what they do." And they parted his raiment and cast lots.

Luke 23:34

The early believers were glad to suffer as Jesus had suffered because they were counted worthy.

And they departed from the presence of the council, rejoicing that they were counted worthy to suffer shame for his name.

Acts 5:41

Stephen was ready to suffer like Jesus, even to the

point of asking forgiveness for his murderers. Such a forgiving response comes only from the Holy Spirit. The Spirit can also help us respond as Stephen did with love for our enemies.

But I say unto you which hear, Love your enemies, do good to them which hate you. Bless them that curse you, and pray for them which despitefully use you.

Luke 6:27-28

How would you react if someone was hurting you because of what you believed?

There are no recorded instances of prayer addressed directly to the Holy Spirit, but I'm confident that it is appropriate to talk to Him about our service, sorrow, and sanctification being that He is associated with all three. Praying to the Holy Spirit is in the scripture from an indirect perspective. In John 16:17, Jesus told His disciples, "Nevertheless, I tell you the truth. It is expedient for you that I go away for if I go not away, the Comforter will not come unto you. But if I depart, I will send Him unto you." The word Comforter is from the Greek word "Paraclete," meaning someone you call alongside to help. Our prayer life must be under the control of the Spirit so that He can pray through us. The Holy Spirit helps us in our distress. We don't even know what we should pray for or how to pray. But the Holy Spirit prays for us with groaning that cannot be expressed in words. And the Father who knows all hearts knows what the Spirit is saying, for the Spirit pleads for us believers in harmony with God's will (Romans 8:26- 27).

Let's understand something about the Holy Spirit. He is referred to as "the one you call alongside." The Holy Spirit helps us in our "infirmities" in our weaknesses. He doesn't leave us alone; we are not abandoned to our petty resources to somehow struggle through all our experiences and live defeated lives. Jesus fully understood this when He got ready to leave this world. He promised that He would not leave His friends alone but would come to them by sending the Comforter, "The Paraclete." (Para) means alongside, and kaleo means to call. When God said, "I will send you a Comforter," He was saying, "I will send you one whom you can call upon who will come alongside and help you with your infirmities."

Let's take a look at the Greek word for "HELP." It is a combination of three words:

SUN meaning along with, together;
ANTI meaning on the opposite side;
LAMBANO meaning to take hold of.

When you put the words together, it is "SUNANTILAMBANOTAI," which means to take hold of together with us over on the other side. Therefore, when Jesus promised to send a Comforter, He promised to send someone who comes alongside us when we call, who will take hold of, together with you, on the other side. It is very helpful to get technical in doing a word analysis, for the word "HELP" in Greek is in the indicative mood and represents a fact. It is in the middle voice, indicating that the Holy Spirit is doing the action; the present tense speaks of habitual, continuous action. The Holy Spirit is always there! One of the great works of comforting counseling is "Paraclete." He is always available to take hold on the other side of our crippling infirmities, our damaged emotions, and our painful hang-ups.

He doesn't leave us because our performance is damaged or imperfect. This verb is found in only one other place in the New Testament. Mary was sitting at the feet of Jesus, enjoying His love and teachings. Martha was hasting about in the kitchen doing all the work by herself. She was also getting more upset by the minute. Finally, she burst through the door onto the front porch where Jesus and Mary were sitting and blurted out, "Jesus, will you please speak to Mary and tell her to come in here and ["SUNANTILAMBANO"] or help me?" (Luke 10:40). Martha was essentially saying, "Tell her to come in here and do her share and get hold of the other side. I can't do it all myself!" That's the picture in this world; the Holy Spirit is helping us, taking hold of the other side.

As a believer, you are not left to your own resources to cope with your problems. Even when you don't know the right words to pray, the Holy Spirit prays with and for you, and God answers. With God helping us to pray, we don't need to be afraid to come before

Him. Ask the Holy Spirit to intercede for you "in harmony with God's will." Then, when you bring your requests to God, trust that He will always do what is best.

The prescribed way to pray is in the Spirit, through the Son, to the Father. Praying in the Divine Name means pleading for the merit, power, and work that the name represents. In the Name (singular form) indicates the unity of the (Godhead) of the Father and of the Son and of the Holy Spirit. Let's trace the use of the Name in scripture.

On judgment day many will tell me, 'Lord, Lord, we prophesied in your name and cast out demons in your name and performed many miracles in your name.' Jesus is going to say to them, "Depart from me. Your work was of iniquity.

Matthew 7:22-23

What is the meaning of this? "Your work was not for me but for you. You tried to use my name to make yourself look good. What you were doing was more about you than me." One cannot use Jesus' name as a magic wand. In biblical days, names depicted character; in my name, in my character. Jesus says that no man cometh unto the Father but by Him. We have narrowed that down to mean salvation, but it means in any respect, especially prayer. I have heard well-worded prayers that were closed just by saying "Amen." The petitioner did not close the prayer by

147

saying, "In Jesus' Name." I believe that unless you say "In Jesus' Name," that prayer stays on Earth. It does not ascend to the throne of God. In the book of Acts, we have a case where some men tried to use Jesus' name for profit.

Then certain of the vagabond Jews, exorcists, took upon them to call over those which had evil spirits the name of the Lord Jesus, saying, "We adjure you by Jesus whom Paul preaches." And there were seven sons of one Sceva, a Jew and chief of the priests, which did so. And the evil spirit answered and said, "Jesus I know, and Paul I know; but who are ye?" And the man in whom the evil spirit was leaped on them, and overcame them, and prevailed against them, so that they fled out of that house naked and wounded. And this was known to all the Jews and Greeks also dwelling at Ephesus, and fear fell on them all, and the name of the Lord Jesus was magnified.

Acts 19:13-17

These Jews traveled from town to town, making a living by claiming to heal people and drive out demons. Often they would recite a whole list of names in their incantation to be sure of including the right deity. They were trying to use Jesus' name to match Paul's power. Many Ephesians engaged in exorcism and occult practices for profit. The sons of Sceva were impressed by Paul, whose power to drive out demons came from God's Holy Spirit, not from witchcraft, and was more powerful than theirs. They discovered, however, that no one can control or duplicate God's power. These men were calling on the name of Jesus without knowing Him personally. The power to change people comes from Christ. It cannot be accessed by reciting His name like a magic charm. God works His power only through those whom He chooses. While teaching the disciples, Jesus says:

I tell you this. If two of you agree down here on Earth concerning anything you ask, my Father in heaven will do it for you. For where two or three gather together because they are mine, I am there among them.

Matthews 18:19-20

Now in keeping this in context, this has to do with church discipline, of which we do very little for fear of what the people will say and fear of losing church members. Jesus also looked ahead to a new day when He would be present with His followers not in body but through His Holy Spirit. In the body of believers (the church), the sincere agreement of two people in prayer is more powerful than the superficial agreement of thousands because Christ's Holy Spirit is with them. Two or more believers, filled with the Holy Spirit, will pray according to God's will and not their own; thus, their requests will be granted. God's word says that you can ask for anything in His name, and He will do it because the work of the Son brings glory to the Father. Take John 14:14, which says, "Yes, ask anything in my name, and I will do it!" When Jesus says that we can ask for anything, we must remember that our asking must be in His name, that is, according to God's character and will. God will not grant requests contrary to His nature or will, and we cannot use His name as a magic formula to fulfill our selfish desires. If we are sincerely following God and seeking to do His will, then our requests will be in line with what He wants, and He will grant them. Jesus looked ahead to that new day.

At that time, you won't need to ask me for anything. The truth is, you can go directly to the Father and ask Him, and He will grant your request because you use my name. You haven't done this before. Ask, using my name, and you will receive, and you will have abundant joy. I have spoken of these matters in parables, but the time will come when this will not be necessary, and I will tell you plainly all about the Father. Then you will ask in my name. I'm not saying I will ask the Father on your behalf, for the Father himself loves you dearly because you love me and believe that I came from God.

John 16:23-27

Jesus is talking about a new relationship between the believer and God. Previously, people approached God through priests. After Jesus' resurrection, any believer could approach God directly. A new day has dawned, and now all believers are priests, talking with God personally. We approach God not because of our own merit but because Jesus, our great High Priest, has made us acceptable to God. But Peter said in Acts 3:6, "I don't have any money for you. But I'll give you what I have. In the name of Jesus Christ of Nazareth, get up and walk!"

In the name of Jesus Christ means by the authority of Jesus Christ. The apostles could do their healing through the Holy Spirit's power, not their own. We are to give thanks in Jesus' name. And you will always give thanks for everything to God the Father in the name of our Lord Jesus Christ, according to Ephesians 5:20. The use of the Divine Name implies a frame of mind rather than a form of speech. I believe one can say the name out of habit without their mind thinking of Jesus; if so, it will be like walking up to a door and just standing there. I teach that a prayer never leaves Earth and never ascends to the throne before God if it is not closed *In Jesus' Name.* Let's look at Peter's statement in Acts 3:16.

The name of Jesus has healed this man, and you know how lame he was before. Faith in Jesus' name has caused this healing before your very eyes.

Jesus, not the apostles, received the glory for the healing of the lame man. By using Jesus' name, Peter showed who gave him the authority and power to heal. The apostles did not emphasize what they could do but what God would do through them. Jesus' name must be used in faith. When we pray in Jesus' name, we must remember that Christ gives our prayers their power, not merely the sound of His name. But what exactly does it mean to pray in the all-prevailing name? Certainly, it does not imply the repetition of a phrase, with no more relationship to the prayer offered as a label has to the parcel it is on. *In His Name*, loosely added to a prayer, does not convert an unholy desire to a worthy one. The phrase is not a cheap servomechanism to open a door in heaven for those who use it. *For Christ's Sake* or *In His Name* indicates the key to the true motive in prayer. The phrases mean that Christ is Lord of our prayer life and that our prayers must have His sanction in advance before He can endorse them for payment by God. The use of the words implies that we are praying as He would pray if in our place. *In His Name* signifies *In His Nature,* according to all He is within Himself and all He has accomplished. Prayer offered for Christ's sake or in His stead will not fail. As we use the phrase, prayer will be unavailing if we are un-Christ-like. I'm not speaking in the ultimate, but in the secondary, for He will hear the sinner's prayer seeking a relationship with Him. We must have His mind.

Let this mind be in you which was also in Christ Jesus.
Philippians 2:5

Your attitude should be the same that Christ Jesus had. Jesus Christ was humble and willing to give up his rights to obey God and serve people. Like Christ, we should have a servant's attitude, serving out of love for God and others, not out of guilt or fear. Remember, you can choose your attitude. You can approach life expecting to be served or look for opportunities to serve others. We must have His mind, correspondence with His will, and harmony with His wishes. As we give Him the right of way in our lives, our prayers find the right of way in God's providence. Just as Christ was assured that His prayer was answered, He professed His thankful acceptance of this answer. He says, "I thank thee that thou has heard me." Though the miracle was not yet wrought, the prayer was answered, and he triumphed before the victory. No other can pretend to have such an assurance as Christ had. Yet we may, by faith in the promise, have a prospect of mercy before it is given and may rejoice in that prospect and give God thanks for it.

Thanking Him before it happens doesn't make it happen. You can't make yourself believe it into happening. I have tried it without fully grasping what Jesus says. He didn't say thank you for the answer as we have taken Him to be saying. He says thank you that thou has heard me. He could say that because He asks according to the will of God, which is the Word of God, and God will always hear when a prayer incorporates the Word of God; in fact, that is genuine prayer. In David's devotions, the same psalms that begin with prayer for mercy close with thanksgiving. Note that mercies, in answer to prayer, should be acknowledged with thankfulness in a special manner. Besides, in granting mercy itself, we are to value it as a great favor to have our poor prayers taken notice of. We ought to meet the first appearances of the return of prayer with early thanksgivings. As God answers us with mercy, even before we call, and hears while we are yet speaking, that is the greatness of God. There is none like Him. We have mistakenly taken it that since that's the way that He is, it is the way we ought to be, but not so. We must do a lot of growing to exercise the kind of faith to praise even before He grants. And to give Him thanks while He is yet speaking is to apply the Word of God that fits your particular situation, knowing that He cannot lie, but you don't know when the prayer will be answered.

A theologian named Dr. R. A. Torrey stated that to pray in the name of Jesus Christ is to recognize that we have no claims on God. He points out that God owes us nothing, and we deserve nothing from God. But believing what God Himself tells us about Jesus Christ's claim upon Him, we ask God for things on the ground of Jesus Christ's claim upon God. I like these statements by Torrey, and the Spirit moved me to analyze them. Through meditation and much searching, I came up with the following claims of Jesus upon God. The Father and I are one (John 10:30), meaning Jesus and his Father are not the same person but one in essence and nature. Thus, Jesus is not merely a good teacher; He is God. His claim to be God was unmistakable. John shows Jesus as fully human and fully God. Although Jesus took upon himself full humanity and lived as a man, he never ceased to be the eternal God who has always existed, the Creator and Sustainer of all things, and the source of eternal life. This is the truth about Jesus and the foundation of all truth. If we cannot believe this basic truth, we will not have enough faith to trust our eternal destiny to Him. The oneness of the nature of Father and Son is that they are the same in substance and equal in power and glory. This is why John wrote his Gospel to build faith and confidence in Jesus Christ so that we may believe He was and is the Son of God.

Jesus says in John 11:42, "And I know that thou hearest me always." This claim is to be a mental state of our exemplifying His character. He had a cheerful assurance of a ready answer at any time. Now let none of us think that this was some uncommon favor granted only to Him such as He never had before, nor should ever have again. No, He had the same divine power going along with Him in his whole undertaking, and He undertook nothing but what He knew to be agreeable to the counsel of God's will. Another claim Jesus has upon God is that He is the door to the Father. He says in John 14:6, "I am the way, the truth, and the life. No one can come to the Father except through me." As the way, Jesus is our path to the Father. As the truth, He is the reality of all God's promises. As the life, He joins his divine life to ours, both now and eternally. In John 14:9, Phillip asks the question to Jesus, "Show us the Father?" Jesus is the visible, tangible image of the invisible God. He is the complete revelation of what God is like. Jesus explained to Philip, who wanted to see the Father, that to know Jesus is to know God. The search for God, for truth and reality, ends in Christ. Another claim of Jesus is in John 14:13. Jesus Christ clarifies that the Father is glorified in the Son.

All I have is yours, and all you have is mine. And glory has come to me through them.

John 17:10

What did Jesus mean when He said, "They are my glory?" God's glory is the revelation of His character and presence. The lives of Jesus' disciples reveal His character, and He is present to the world through them. Does your life reveal Jesus' character and presence? The disciples knew the power of praying in the Divine Name. We must do something so that we may reap God's bounty; we must call upon Him. He will be enquired of, and surely that which is not worth the asking is not worth the having. We have nothing to do but walk in prayer to God. What is the life of a Christian but a life of prayer? It implies a sense of our dependence on Him, an entire dedication of ourselves to Him, and a believing expectation of our all from Him.

Some have argued that Old Testament saints prayed directly to God and that prayer is made poorer if we now have to come to God indirectly through a mediator. All we seek in prayer must be for the glory of the Divine Name. If our prayers are self-weighted, they will never rise very high. All selfish or unworthy desires must be shunned. The spirit of any prayer must be "Thine is the glory." I have grown in my prayer life to the point of knowing that when I wrap myself up with God and His concerns, He will wrap Himself up in what concerns me, always doing what is best for me.

In my being a pastor for 40 years, I have been bringing the congregation up for what is called "Altar Prayer." The people were coming up before the pulpit for prayer, and I was praying from behind the pulpit for them. In the second church that I pastored, the Oak Hill Baptist Church, it dawned on me that the pulpit was not an altar but a pulpit. Therefore when we came before Christ for an altar call, I came down out of the pulpit on the floor with the congregation to lead us all in prayer before Christ.

There were questions about this practice until they experienced the difference. It became more reverent with us all standing before Christ in prayer. I took the same practice to the third church that I pastored, Cumberland Baptist Church. Perhaps this is why the Lord gave us an actual altar to go before, the "Altar of Seven Bibles," sitting beside the pulpit at Rehoboth Baptist Church. Each Sunday morning, I bring the congregation before the altar, and I pray for them, and since the church has about five associate ministers, we all get a chance to go before the altar. The congregation of Rehoboth has been taught not to bring their problems to God but to bring themselves according to the Word of God.

I beseech you therefore, brethren, by the mercies of God, that ye present your bodies a living sacrifice, holy, acceptable unto God, which is your reasonable service. And be not conformed to this world: but be ye transformed by the renewing of your mind, that ye may prove what is that good, and acceptable, and perfect, will of God.

Romans 12:1-2

The congregation is told that God already knows what they are going through, and the way to get God involved to help them is to wrap themselves up with what concerns the Lord, and He will, in turn, wrap Himself up in what concern us because He does not want it hindering us in our service to Him. They get their problems prayed for, but it is done as an intercessory prayer through me as pastor or the associate minister praying that Sunday. Traditionally congregations are brought up selfishly, and it is all about them and not Christ and His work through His body in the church. We now pray for Him to use us in His service to His glory because He is a spirit and needs to be personified and given visibility.

PRAYING IN THE SPIRIT

Knowing how to pray in the Spirit is vital to our prayer lives.

But ye, beloved, building up yourselves on your most holy faith, praying in the Holy Ghost.

Jude 1:20

This verse marks the majestic characteristic of true prayer—"In the Holy Ghost." The seed of acceptable devotion must come from heaven's storehouse. Only the prayer which comes from God can go to God. We must shoot the Lord's arrows back to Him. That desire He writes upon our heart will move His heart and bring down a blessing, but the desires of the flesh have no power with Him. Praying in the Holy Ghost is praying in fervency. Cold prayers ask the Lord not to hear them. Those who do not plead with fervency plead not at all. As well speak of lukewarm fire as of lukewarm prayer—it is essential that it be red hot. It is praying perseveringly. The true suppliant gathers force as he proceeds and grows more fervent when God delays answering. The longer the gate is closed, the more vehemently he uses the knocker. The longer the angel lingers, the more resolved he is that he will never let him go without the blessing.

Beautiful in God's sight is tearful, agonizing, unconquerable persistence. It means praying humbly, for the Holy Spirit never puffs us up with pride. It is His office to convince us of sin, and so to bow us down in contrition and brokenness of spirit. We shall never sing "Glory, Hallelujah!" except we pray to God profoundly; out of the depths must we cry, or we shall never behold glory in the highest. It is loving prayer. Prayer should be perfumed with love, saturated with love—love to our fellow saints and love to Christ.

Moreover, it must be a prayer full of faith. A man only prevails as he believes. The Holy Spirit is the author of faith and strengthens it so that we pray to believe God's promise. O, that this blessed combination of excellent graces, priceless and sweet as the spices of the merchant, might be fragrant within us because the Holy Ghost is in our hearts! We should cry earnestly, "Most blessed Comforter, exert Thy mighty power within us, helping our infirmities in prayer!"

Pray at all times and on every occasion in the power of the Holy Spirit. Praying always with all prayer and supplications in the Spirit, and watching thereunto with all perseverance and supplications for all the saints.

Ephesians 6:18

Stay alert and be persistent in your prayers for all Christians everywhere. Note the kind of prayer this is for all Christians. It is intercessory praying. How can a person pray at all times? One way is to make quick, brief prayers your habitual response to every situation you meet throughout the day. Another way is to order your life around God's desires and teachings so that your very life becomes a prayer. You don't have to isolate yourself from other people and daily work to pray constantly. You can make prayer your life and your life a prayer while living in a world that needs God's powerful influence.

We also should pray for all believers in Christ, so pray for the Christians you know, and pray for the churches worldwide, and the Holy Spirit will help us in our distress. Note how you get the Holy Spirit's help—intercessory praying.

For we don't even know what we should pray for, nor how we should pray. But the Holy Spirit prays for us with groaning that cannot be expressed in words. And the Father who knows all hearts knows what the Spirit is saying, for the Spirit pleads for the believers in harmony with God's own will.

Romans 8:26-27

The misunderstanding of this passage of scripture has caused many to be lazy when it comes to prayer, not realizing that true genuine prayer is laborious. Many think it is unnecessary to spend time with God in meditation, thinking and seeking to pray according to His will as written in the Word. Many just give God a quick prayer so they can give their mind to worldliness, gratifying the flesh, having no time for God. However, many seek to find their situation in scripture and pray accordingly. We think we can say a few words, and the Holy Spirit will do the rest with groaning that cannot be uttered.

Paul was teaching that the Holy Spirit only intercedes with groaning when you are praying for something "in harmony with God's own will." So then, when you bring your requests to God, trust that he will always do what is best. According to Philippians 4:6, "Don't worry about anything; instead, pray about everything." Tell God what you need, and thank Him for all He has done. Imagine never worrying about anything! It seems like it is impossible. We all have worries on the job, in our homes, at school, etc. But Paul's advice is to turn our worries into prayers. Do you want to worry less? Then pray more! Whenever you start to worry, stop and pray. We must devote ourselves to prayer with an alert mind and a thankful heart. Paul wrote to the church at Colossi, asking the church not to forget to pray for them. He asked the church to pray that God would give them many opportunities to preach about

His secret plan that Christ is also for the Gentiles, for that was why he was in chains (Colossians 4:2-4).

Have you ever grown tired of praying for something or someone? Paul says we should "devote" ourselves to prayer and be "alert" in prayer. Our persistence is an expression of our faith that God answers our prayers. We don't persist in prayer in order to get from God; we persist because we are getting something from prayer. You are in the company of God, and being in the company of one that you love sharing with is very consoling. We must also know that persistence is an expression that honors God, and He will answer. In reality, one only keeps doing something because they are getting something out of it; otherwise, they will quit. If you start praying and quit, you haven't experienced the joy of His company. When you are praying in the Spirit, faith doesn't die if the answers come slowly, for the delay may be God's way of working His will in your life. When you feel tired of praying, strengthen yourself in knowing that God is present, always listening, always answering, maybe not in ways you had hoped, but in ways that He knows are best. One sure way to get God's ear is to talk to one another about Him.

Then they that feared the LORD spoke often one to another; and the LORD hearkened, and heard it. And a book of remembrance was written before him for them that feared the LORD, and that thought upon his name. 'And they shall be mine,' saith the LORD of hosts, 'in that day when I make up my jewels; and I will spare them, as a man spared his own son that serves him.' Then shall ye return, and discern between the righteous and the wicked, between him that serves God and him that serves him not.

Malachi 3:16-18

Realize, dear reader, that if you want God's attention, strike up a conversation with someone over Him; the Word of God says that He hearkens. In other words, He tunes in to the conversation. You may be talking to one, but two are listening—the one you are talking to and God. Paul wanted the people to know that there was a "secret plan," which was Christ's Good News of Salvation. The whole focus of Paul's life was to tell others about Christ, explaining and preaching this wonderful mystery. He asked for them to pray that he would proclaim this message as clearly as he should.

Paul wanted prayer for himself, and so did I as I wrote this book. But how many of us pray that God will open the people's hearts (minds) to the pastor's message that he preaches on Sunday mornings? It is a prayer that will be heard and answered because it is according to His will.

And this is the confidence that we have in him that, if we ask any thing according to his will he heareth us. And if we know that he hears us, whatsoever we ask, we know that we have the petitions that we desired of him.

I John 5:14-15

The Word of God is the will of God. Pray according to His Will. The book of Acts tells us about a woman named Lydia who was converted under Paul.

And a certain woman named Lydia, a seller of purple, of the city of Thyatira, which worshipped God, heard us; whose heart the Lord opened, that she attended unto the things which were spoken of Paul.

Acts 16:14

Right here, let me share with pastors and teachers of the Word of God. If you want to see growth and development in the lives of the people to whom you preach and teach, then pray Acts 16:14 back to God. Remind God that He opened Lydia's heart. He loves to be reminded of what He has said and done. It honors Him, not that He has forgotten, for He is omniscient (He is all-knowing). He wants you to remind Him of what He says for you so that you are confident of what He has said.

At Rehoboth Baptist Church, I have been able to experience Paul's joy. He says to the church in Rome that his joy is their growth in the Lord, and so it is with me. He has enabled me to see growth in some of the members of Rehoboth. I wish it was all, but unfortunately, it is not. Paul asked for prayer that he could proclaim the Good News about Christ clearly, and we should request prayer to do the same. No matter what approach to evangelism we use, whether emphasizing lifestyle, example or building relationships, we should never obscure the message of the Good News.

I personally believe that a sermon that is not tied to the death, burial, resurrection, ascension, and return of the Lord is only a message of good advice -- a lot of true things said without application because Christ did all that we teach or preach. Everything in the Old or 1st Testament points to Christ, then everything in the 2nd or New Testament points back to Christ.

But you, dear friends, must continue to build your lives on the foundation of your holy faith, and continue to pray as you are directed by the Holy Spirit.

Jude 1:20

To pray as we are "directed by the Holy Spirit" means to pray in the power and strength of the Holy Spirit. He prays for us, opens our minds to Jesus, and teaches us about Him. Pray in the Holy Ghost. We all need to know this, and I have come to realize that prayer is the nurse of faith; the way to build ourselves in our most holy faith is to continue in prayer. What is the role of a nurse? They are caretakers. Our prayers are then most likely to prevail when we pray in the Holy Ghost, that is, under His guidance and influence.

Howbeit when he, the Spirit of truth, is come, he will guide you into all truth: for he shall not speak of himself; but whatsoever he shall hear, that shall he speak: and he will show you things to come. He shall glorify me; for he shall receive of mine, and shall show it unto you. All things that the Father hath are mine: therefore said I, that he shall take of mine, and shall show it unto you.

John 16:13-15

Here are words that do away with praying in what many call "speaking in tongues," saying that the Holy Spirit is doing it. If He did, He would be calling attention to Himself, for Jesus never spoke in tongues. Therefore it is a misunderstanding that the Holy Spirit causes one to speak in a babbling language. I had an experience with a coworker about speaking in tongues when I was working at Dover Corporation. Another person heard our conversation and involved himself by sharing that he was at a church, and they were "speaking in tongues." This person understood the language in which they were speaking, and he stated that they didn't know what they were saying because they were cursing God instead of blessing God. One leaves himself open for Satan to take advantage of them when they don't understand what they are saying.

Paul asks the people to pray that God would give him the right words as he boldly explains God's secret plan that the Good News is for the Gentiles too. He was in chains for preaching that message as God's ambassador. He was persecuted for preaching the truth, and the day is coming when we are going to experience the same. He said to them to keep praying that he would keep speaking boldly for Him, as he should.

Undiscouraged and undefeated, Paul wrote powerful letters of encouragement from prison. Church members should pray for their pastor the same way. Paul did not ask the Ephesians to pray that his chains would be removed but that he would continue to speak fearlessly for Christ in spite of them. God can use us in any circumstance to do His will. Note the frame of mind Paul is in as he prays not to be delivered from his chains but that God will be blessed while he is in chains. Even as we pray for a change in our circumstances, we should also pray that God would accomplish His plan through us right where we are. Knowing God's eternal purpose for us will help us through difficult times. The Holy Spirit must pray in and through us. It is He who helps our weakness in prayer and makes our intercession to the will of God.

For those who are living in the way of the flesh give their minds to the things of the flesh, but those who go in the way of the Spirit, to the things of the Spirit. Know something about God as it relates to your mind. For the mind of the flesh is death, but the mind of the Spirit is life and peace. Because the mind of the flesh is opposed to God, it is not under the law of God and is not able to be. So that those who are in the flesh are not able to give pleasure to God. You are not in the flesh but in the Spirit if the Spirit of God is in you. But if any man has not the Spirit of Christ, he is not one of His.

Romans 8:5-9

Here Paul divides people into two categories: those who let themselves be controlled by their sinful nature and those who follow after the Holy Spirit. All of us would be in the first category if Jesus didn't offer us a way out. Thank God for His coming, going to Calvary, dying for our sins, being buried, rising on the third day, going out on the Mount of Olives, ascending back to heaven, and the angels saying, "Why stand here gazing? The same way you see Him going, He is coming back." Once we have said yes to Jesus, we will want to continue following Him because His way brings life and peace. Daily we must consciously choose to center our lives on God. Use the Bible to discover God's guidelines and then follow them. In every perplexing situation, ask yourself, "What would Jesus want me to do?"

When the Holy Spirit points out what is right, do it eagerly. Have you ever worried about whether or not you really are a Christian? I was led to teach the church I serve and my radio broadcast that it is one thing for others or yourself to say you are a child of

God. But has He told you, "You are my child?" We need to hear from Him because others will deceive us, and we will lie to ourselves.

A Christian is anyone who has the Spirit of God living in them. If you have sincerely trusted Christ for your salvation and acknowledged Him as Lord, then the Holy Spirit takes up residence in you, leading you to become a Christian disciple. Consider the Word Christian; the "ian" at the end of the word is a participle meaning you are a part of the property of the proper noun Christ. You can be assured that you have the Holy Spirit because Jesus promised that he would send him. Since you now believe that Jesus Christ is God's Son and that eternal life comes through him, you will begin to act as Christ directs. One way to be sure He will direct you is coming to teaching being a disciple. Find a church where the pastor doesn't mind you asking questions, for that is the only way you are going to get an understanding and find help in your daily problems and your prayer life. You will be empowered to serve God and do His will. You will become part of God's plan to build His church.

It's God the Spirit who induces true prayer in the heart (mind). We pray in the Spirit through the merits of Christ to the Father. To pray in the spirit means consciously placing ourselves under the Holy Spirit's influence. When you do this, He will lead you into prayer according to His will. He makes our conscience sensitive to sin and inspires prayers God delights to listen to. A theologian by the name of Andrew Murray has given us this pregnant thought: The Spirit breathing, the Son's intercession, and the Father's will. These three become one in us when we pray.

POSTURES IN PRAYER

There are many postures in prayer. The ones most commonly used are bowing on one knee or both knees and standing with the bowing of the head. That is just three out of many others, and I have been led to use some of them that are not commonly used. I will reveal them as we discuss this topic.

And the people believed: and when they heard that the LORD had visited the children of Israel and that he had looked upon their affliction, then they bowed their heads and worshipped.

Exodus 4:31

When did the bowing take place? It was when the children of Israel realized God had looked upon their affliction. It is the celebration of the Lord's Passover, for He passed over the homes of the Israelites in Egypt. And though He killed the Egyptians, He spared our families and did not destroy us.

Then all the people bowed their heads and worshiped.

Exodus 12:27

They bowed their heads when they had been spared.

Then the servant bowed his head and he said, Blessed be the Lord God of my master Abraham, who hath not left destitute my master of his mercy and his truth: I being in the way, the Lord led me to the house of my master's brethren.

Genesis 24:26-27

When Solomon finished praying and making his requests to the Lord, he stood up in front of the altar of the Lord, where he had been kneeling with his hands raised toward heaven. Note what Solomon prayed; Solomon praised the Lord and prayed for the people. He stood there and shouted this blessing over the entire community of Israel. (I Kings 8:54-55) It is called his blessing of the people. His prayer can be a pattern for our prayers. When one reads this, you will see that he had five basic requests:

1. For God's presence. The LORD our God be with us, as he was with our fathers: let him not leave us, nor forsake us (I King 8:57)
2. For the desire to do God's will in everything
3. For the desire and ability to obey God's commands that He may incline our hearts unto Him, to walk in all His ways, and to keep His

commandments, and His statutes, and His judgments, which He commanded our fathers? (I Kings 8:58)

4. He prayed for help with each day's needs, saying: And let these my words, wherewith I have made supplication before the Lord be nigh unto the Lord our God day and night, that he maintain the cause of his servant, and the cause of his people Israel at all times, as the matter shall require (I King 8:59)

5. He prayed for the spread of God's Kingdom to the entire world. That all the people of the earth may know that the Lord is God and that there is none else (I King 8:60).

Please note the request of Solomon. He prayed God-weighted and not self-weighted prayers. He prayed for that which would bring God honor. Matthew 6:33 says, "Seek ye first the kingdom of heaven and its righteousness, and all these things shall be added." I taught my congregation that there is nothing that concerns us that is not included in *these things*. They would be added if we just seek the kingdom of God first. Most of the prayers that we pray concern us and not the things of God. Thank God for spiritual growth in Him. I have personally grown in Him because my prayer life has been revolutionized to the extent that I'm able to show it to the congregation that I serve. Our prayers need to be weighted down with God's concerns. My former secretary, the late Ruth Maddox, put two sayings in our church bulletin concerning kneeling, and I like them. One said that a lot of kneeling will keep you standing, and the other said that prayer doesn't give God instructions; it is just to report for duty.

Solomon made a bronze platform 7 1/2 feet long, 7 1/2 feet wide, and 4 1/2 feet high and placed it at the center of the Temple's outer courtyard (2 Chronicles 6:13). He stood on the platform before the entire assembly and then he knelt down and lifted his hands toward heaven. I did about a year of study on prayer. When it came to altar calls, the people always stood during prayer, but since the teaching, I have taken the whole congregation down on their knees in prayer as I was moved upon. The Prophet Ezra gives us more about this posture in prayer.

At the time of the sacrifice, I stood up from where I had sat in mourning with my clothes torn. I fell to my knees and lifted my hands to the Lord my God after learning about the sins of the people.

Ezra 9:5

Ezra fell to his knees in prayer. He put himself into the posture of a penitent humbling himself and a petitioner appealing for mercy. In both ways, he represented the people for whom he was now an intercessor. He spread out his hands, as one affected by what he was going to say, offering it up unto God, waiting, and reaching out, as it were, with an earnest expectation to receive a gracious answer. This lets us know that our gesture means something to God. In this, he had an eye toward God as the Lord and as his God, a God of power, but a God of grace. His heartfelt prayer provides a good perspective on sin. He recognized that sin is serious, that no one sins without affecting others, that he was not sinless (although he didn't have a pagan wife), and that God's love and mercy had spared the nation when they did nothing to deserve it. It is easy to view sin lightly in a world that sees sin as inconsequential, but we should view sin as seriously as Ezra did. The prophet Daniel also gives us a posture of prayer.

But when Daniel learned that the law had been signed, he went home and knelt down as usual in his upstairs room, with its windows open toward Jerusalem. He prayed three times a day, just as he had always done, giving thanks to his God.

Daniel 6:10

Daniel stood alone. Although he knew about the law against praying to anyone except the king, he continued to pray three times a day as he always had. Daniel had a disciplined prayer life to the extent that nothing stopped him from praying. Our prayers are usually interrupted, not by threats, but simply by the pressure of our schedules. Don't let threats or pressures cut into your prayer time. Pray regularly, no matter what, for prayer is your lifeline to God. Daniel's constant practice was the general practice of the religious Jews. Cornelius was a man who prayed in his house (Acts 10:30). Note that every house ought to be a house of prayer where we should have our own altar, for God must have an altar, and on it, we must offer spiritual sacrifices. Cornelius gave thanks in every prayer. When we pray to God for the mercies we want, we must praise Him for those we have received. Thanksgiving must be a part of every prayer. In his prayer and thanksgiving, Cornelius had an eye toward God as his God. God was his in covenant, and he set himself as always being in His presence. He did this before his God and with regard to Him.

When Daniel prayed and gave thanks, he knelt upon his knees, which is the most proper gesture in prayer and the most expressive of humility, reverence, and submission to God. Kneeling is a begging posture, and we come to God as beggars, beggars for our lives, and it behooves us to be persistent. When Jesus said in Matthew 7:7, "Ask" and it shall be given, "Seek" and ye shall find, "Knock" and the door shall be open to you," all three of these verbs (ask, seek, and knock) are in the Greek present tense which means continuous. And more specifically, the word "Ask" in Greek also means to "beg."

And he was withdrawn from them about a stone's cast, and kneeled down, and prayed, Saying, Father, if thou be willing, remove this cup from me: nevertheless not my will, but thine, be done.

Luke 22:41-42

Was Jesus trying to get out of his mission? The principle here is that it is never wrong to express our true feelings to God. Jesus exposed His dread of the coming trials, but He also reaffirmed His commitment to do what God wanted. The cup that He spoke of meant the terrible agony He knew He would endure— not only the horror of the crucifixion but, even worse, the total separation from God that He would have to experience in order to die for the sins of the world. He who knew no sin or what it was like to be separated from His Father would experience something that He knew nothing about. Take a look at yourself at this junction. Think of someone you care a lot about and imagine that all of a sudden, that person can't have anything else to do with you anymore. How would you feel?

Another posture in prayer is given to us by Stephen.

And he fell to his knees, shouting, 'Lord, don't charge them with this sin!

Acts 7:60

We also see in the scriptures that before Peter healed Tabitha, he took the posture of kneeling.

But Peter asked them all to leave the room; then he knelt and prayed. Turning to the body, he said, 'Get up, Tabitha.' And she opened her eyes! When she saw Peter, she sat up!

Acts 9:40

There is yet another posture that will get God's attention. It is called "on your face before God." Now this posture is not a regularly used posture.

And it came to pass, when the congregation was gathered against Moses and against Aaron that they looked toward the tabernacle of the congregation: And, behold, the cloud covered it, and the glory of the Lord appeared. And Moses and Aaron came before the tabernacle of the congregation. "And the Lord spoke unto Moses, saying get you up from among this congregation, that I may consume them as in a moment. And they fell upon their faces.

Numbers 16:44-45

When it comes to the posture of being on your face before God, there are many examples of this taking place in the lives of persons during times when God showed up unexpectedly. The Word of God says, "And when Abram was ninety years old and nine, the Lord appeared to Abram, and said unto him, I am the Almighty God; walk before me, and be thou perfect. And I will make my covenant between me and thee and will multiply thee exceedingly. And Abram fell on his face: and God talked with him." (Genesis 17:1-3) The falling of Abram on his face while God talked with him was the attitude of the most profound reverence assumed by Eastern people. It consists of the prostrate body stretched out flat with the face and the forehead touching the ground. It was an expression of conscious humility and deep reverence. This comes about when one considers how wretched they are, being self-conscious of the honors done to one so unworthy. To put it another way, you will look upon yourself with humility and upon God with reverence, and, in token of both, you will fall on your face in self-abasement of your own un-deservedness of such favors in your reverence and worship of God.

The Bible gives us another example of going face down before God when you realize that He is near. This happened to Balaam when he allowed himself to be hired to go and curse the Israelites.

And God's anger was kindled because he went: and the angel of the Lord stood in the way for an adversary against him. Now he was riding upon his ass [donkey] and his two servants were with him. And the [donkey] saw the angel of the Lord standing in the way, and his sword drawn in his hand: and the [donkey] turned aside out of the way, and went into the field: and Balaam smote the [donkey], to turn her into the way. But the angel of the Lord stood in a path of the vineyards, a wall being on this side and a wall on that side. And when the [donkey] saw the angel of the Lord, she thrust herself unto the wall, and crushed Balaam's foot against the wall: and he smote her again. And the angel of the Lord went further and stood in a narrow place, where was no way to turn either to the right hand or to the left. And when the [donkey] saw the angel of the Lord, she fell down under Balaam: and Balaam's anger was kindled, and he smote the [donkey] with a staff. And the Lord opened the mouth of the [donkey], and she said unto Balaam, 'What have I done unto thee, that thou hast smitten me these three times?' And Balaam said unto the [donkey], 'Because thou hast mocked me: I would there were a sword in mine hand, for now would I kill thee.' And the [donkey] said unto Balaam, 'Am not I thine [donkey], upon which thou hast ridden ever since I was thine unto this day? Was I ever want to do so unto thee?' And he said, 'nay.' Then the Lord opened the eyes of Balaam, and he saw the angel of the Lord standing in the way, and his sword drawn in his hand: and he bowed down his head, and fell flat on his face.

Numbers 22:22-31

Falling face down speaks of the intensity and the urgency of the matter, the seriousness of it. It was also an experience of Joshua, the successor of Moses. It is found in Joshua 5.

And it came to pass, when Joshua was by Jericho, that he lifted up his eyes and looked, and, behold, there stood a man over against him with his sword drawn in his hand: and Joshua went unto him, and said unto him, 'Art thou for us, or for our adversaries?' And he said, 'Nay; but as captain of the host of the Lord am I now come.' And Joshua fell on his face to the earth, and did worship, and said unto him, 'What saith my lord unto his servant?' And the captain of the Lord's host said unto Joshua, 'Lose thy shoe from off thy foot; for the place whereon thou standest is holy.' And Joshua did so.

Joshua 5:13-15

Joshua was general of the forces of Israel, yet he was far from looking with jealousy upon this stranger, who produced a commission as captain of the Lord's host above him. He did not offer to dispute his claims but cheerfully submitted to him as his commander. The posture of falling on one's face before God is also used when one is deeply seeking a blessing from God.

And it came to pass, when he was in a certain city, behold a man full of leprosy: who seeing Jesus fell on his face, and besought him, saying, 'Lord, if thou wilt, thou canst make me clean.

Luke 5:12

The posture of falling on one's face before God is used in one expressing sincere gratitude to God for hearing and answering their prayers.

And one of them, when he saw that he was healed, turned back, and with a loud voice glorified God, and fell down on his face at his feet, giving him thanks: and he was a Samaritan.

Luke 17:15-16

The various postures in prayer continue.

So Ahab prepared a feast. But Elijah climbed to the top of Mount Carmel and fell to the ground and prayed.

I Kings 18:42

Then King Jehoshaphat bowed down with his face to the ground. And all the people of Judah and Jerusalem did the same, worshiping the Lord.

2 Chronicles 20:18

And He [Jesus] went on a little farther and fell face down on the ground, praying, 'My Father! If it is possible, let this cup of suffering be taken away from me. Yet I want your will, not mine, to be done.

Matthew 26:39

There are several instructive features in our Savior's prayer in His hour of trial. It was a lonely prayer. He withdrew even from His three favored disciples, Peter, James, and John. Believers, be much in solitary prayer, especially in times of trial. Family prayer, social prayer, and prayer in the Church will not suffice, though they are very precious. But the best-beaten spice will smoke in your censer in your private devotions, where no ear hears but God's. The best prayer is when you only have God as your audience. For Christ, it was humble prayer. Luke says that He knelt, but another evangelist says that He "fell on His face." Where, then, must be our place? What dust and ashes should cover our heads! Humility gives us a good foot-hold in prayer. There is no hope of prevalence with God unless we abase ourselves that He may exalt us in due time. It was filial prayer. "Abba, Father." (Mark 14:36). You will find it a stronghold on the day of trial to plead your adoption. You have no rights on your own; you have forfeited them by your treason, but nothing can forfeit a child's right to a father's protection. Be not afraid to say, "My Father, hear my cry." Observe that it was a persevering prayer. He prayed three times. Cease not until you prevail. Be as the importunate widow in Luke 18 whose continual coming earned what her first supplication could not win. Continue in prayer, and watch in the same with thanksgiving.

Note that Christ's prayer was a prayer of resignation. "...Nevertheless, not as I will, but as thou wilt." (Luke 22:42). When we yield, God yields. Let it be as God wills, and God will determine for the best. Be thou content to keep thy prayer before Him who knows when to give, how to give, what to give, and what to withhold. Therefore pleading, earnestly, importunately, yet with humility and resignation, thou shall surely prevail.

Then Solomon stood with his hands lifted toward heaven before the altar of the Lord in front of the entire community of Israel. He prayed, "O Lord, God of Israel, there is no God like you in all of heaven or earth. You keep your promises and show unfailing love to all that obey you and are eager to do your will.

I Kings 8:22

The exaltation of God always has its place with God. When a person is exalted, most of the time, they are compared to somebody else, but when it comes to God, there is none with whom to compare Him; He stands alone. One has to go high in their vocabulary, as high as they can think, using all the synonyms of words that they can use, and still, you will fall far short of describing Him. Jesus taught in Mark 11:25, "And whenever you stand praying, if you have anything against anyone, forgive him that your Father in heaven may also forgive you your trespasses."

The proud Pharisee stood by himself and prayed this prayer, 'I thank you, God, that I am not a sinner like everyone else, especially like that tax collector over there! For I never cheat, I don't sin, I don't commit adultery, I fast twice a week, and I give you a tenth of my income.' But the tax collector stood at a distance and dared not even to lift his eyes to heaven as he prayed. Instead, he beat his chest in sorrow, saying, 'O God, be merciful to me, for I am a sinner."

Luke 18:11-13

Let me hurry up and testify about the greatest blessing the Lord ever gave me. Though He has blessed me in so many other ways, there is none equal to the one I'm about to share with you. It was my noonday Bible study, and the usual noonday attendees were present, along with Rev. Isaac Curry, who was attending Lane College at that time. Rehoboth had employed him part-time to work with me. While I was teaching the class on prayer, I was making a point on the difference between the way the Pharisees prayed and the way the publican prayed, and all of a sudden, I was stunned. I stood before the class in silence. I couldn't say anything. Tears started flowing down my cheeks. The class was looking on in amazement, and I just burst out sobbing. I went out into the hallway and kept crying out loud.

Rev. Curry came up and kept teaching the class, but they could still hear me in the hallway. When I was able to compose myself, I came back into the class and told them what happened. I told them that the Lord told me that I was the Pharisee because of the way I thought of myself. I had exalted myself in thinking that I was better than other preachers because I knew some of the things that many of them were doing that were not becoming of a preacher, and I was saying to myself, "I'm not like them. I'm better than them. I'm a man of faith, fully committed, faithful to my wife."

And although those things are true, I had the wrong attitude about it. I was disgusting to God, all while I thought I was the best thing going. I was accrediting myself like the Pharisee when I should have had the attitude of the publican, "Lord be merciful unto me, a sinner." I consider it the greatest blessing He ever gave me because He didn't leave me blind to myself. I repented, and He forgave me, and now through the Holy Spirit's help, I maintain the right attitude toward myself, an attitude of humility. The Lord used me to set others free as well. The late Rev. Joseph Mann came and thanked me because I had helped him to see what he needed to do. He did it, and his whole attitude changed in that whereas he was always sad and discouraged, he became cheerful and very pleasant in his spirit. When the Lord called him home, I believe that he was at peace with God.

Being in the Lord's presence and recognizing it will put you on your face. I had to get out of my desk chair one Thursday and go face down on my office floor because He came in so close to me. I was in sermon preparation, and I was searching the Bible for scripture to give support to a thought that the Holy Spirit had brought to mind. I came across a scripture that the Lord used to speak to me about my wretchedness. I saw myself, and His presence was so strong that it prostrated me on the floor face down before Him, saying, "Oh, Lord! Oh, Lord!"

I had gone in for prayer before the visible altar that was erected the night of Rehoboth's first church business meeting, and on this particular day, I was praying for a need so intense that I ended up on my face. I started out standing as I prayed, and then I proceeded to my knees and progressed onto my face with my hands stretched out. What I have discovered is that one has to be moved upon before one ends up on their face in prayer. It is not a position one just takes to pray. God has to put you on your face before Him, and sometimes He does just that. How are we to show respect for God? It is by our attitudes and actions. We should recognize God's power, authority, and deep love, and our actions must model our attitudes before others. Respect for God is just as important today as it was in Joshua's day, even though removing shoes is no longer our cultural way of showing it.

Being in "awe" of God means an emotion in which dread, veneration, and wonder are variously mingled. It is a fearful reverence inspired by a deity or by something sacred or mysterious. It is a submissive and admiring response inspired by authority or power. That is, we should stand in "awe" of God. I want close this chapter on Postures in Prayer by referring back to what Jesus did.

And in the morning, rising up a great while before day, he went out, and departed into a solitary place, and there prayed.

Mark 1:35

The Bible does not specify the posture that He put Himself in as He communed with His Father in that solitary place, but I wonder if it was sitting in deep thought with His Father. I present the sitting posture because it is the posture I use every morning when I rise early and go into another room in the house while others are still asleep and sit in deep thought, in meditational prayer to God. When I finish, I stand and stretch both hands toward heaven and present my body in obedience to the Word.

I beseech you therefore, brethren, by the mercies of God, that ye present your bodies a living sacrifice, holy, acceptable unto God, which is your reasonable service. And be not conformed to this world: but be ye transformed by the renewing of your mind, that ye may prove what is that good, and acceptable, and perfect, will of God.

Romans 12:1-2

UNDERSTANDING REPENTANCE

This study on repentance is very lengthy because of the many questions that were generated due to what the members had heard all of their lives. The people believed that to repent was only to have godly sorrow for what they had done, and they did not understand the process of expressing that sorrow. A disciple in the church named Ms. Stella Shead came to me and said, "Pastor, this is one of the best studies that you have taught!" It was revealed from the study on repentance that it is a subject that has been dealt with very lightly by various religions, but it is imperative with Jesus Christ.

Except you repent you will all likewise perish.

Luke 13:3

This is the negative or judgmental side of Jesus' message. We looked thoroughly at the judgmental side because of the lateness of the hour of our Lord's return.

The word "repent" in its various forms occurs 45 times in the Old Testament and carries the underlying thought of contrition.

For thus saith the high and lofty One that inhabited eternity, whose name is Holy; I dwell in the high and holy place, with him also that is of a contrite and humble spirit, to revive the spirit of the humble, and to revive the heart of the contrite ones.

Isaiah 57:15

For all those things hath mine hand made, and all those things have been, saith the Lord: but to this man will I look, even to him that is poor and of a contrite spirit, and trembled at my word.

Isaiah 66:2

In the New Testament, the word "repent" occurs 61 times with the meaning of thinking differently, that is, to change one's mind. Then, there are related terms to repentance occurring around 600 times. In the New Testament, we see the keynote of John the Baptist's preaching:

Repent, for the kingdom of heaven is at hand.

Matthew 3:2

To the multitudes he declared, "Bring forth fruits worthy of repentance.

Matthew 3:5-9

When Jesus began His ministry, He continued to carry on John's preaching of the message of repentance, expanding the message to include the good news of salvation.

Now after that John was put in prison, Jesus came into Galilee, preaching the gospel of the kingdom of God, and saying, 'The time is fulfilled, and the kingdom of God is at hand: repent ye, and believe the gospel.

Mark 1:14-15

In Jesus' preaching of the kingdom of God, the truth is seen that repentance and faith are two sides of the same coin. By repentance, one turns away from sin; by faith, one turns toward God in accepting the Lord Jesus Christ as Savior. Such a two-fold turning, or conversion, is necessary for entrance into the kingdom.

Verily I say unto you, except ye be converted, and become as little children, ye shall not enter into the kingdom of heaven.

Matthew 18:3

It needs to be realized by all of Christendom that "repent" is as much a command of God as "Thou shalt not steal." (Exodus 20:15). Repentance was not being seen in that light. "Believe on the Lord Jesus Christ" has as much a divine authority as "Thou shalt love the Lord thy God with all thy heart, with all thy soul, with all thy strength." (Deuteronomy 6:5). We are not given the option to repent and believe the gospel; they are commands. But sadly, they have been presented as options when they are not.

Repentance is turning away from sin and dedicating oneself to amending one's life. It is to change one's mind, to cause one to feel regret or contrition. It is a turning away from sin, disobedience, or rebellion and returning to God. Jesus says that He came not to call the righteous but sinners to repentance (Luke 5:32). Several ingredients make up genuine repentance. First of all, there is humiliation revealed in contrition, that is, the breaking of the heart as when a rock is broken. The word of God will do this in your life. He says in Jeremiah 23:29, "Is not my word like as a fire? Saith the Lord; and like a hammer that breaketh the rock in pieces?" The Living Bible Translation says, "Does not my word burn like fire? Asks the Lord. Is it not like a mighty hammer that smashed the rock to pieces?" Now the meaning of the word "contrite" according to the Old or 1st Testament is having a remorseful, repentant, regretful spirit.

The Lord is near to those who have a broken heart, and saves such that have a contrite spirit.

Psalm 34:18

The Life Application Bible says, "The Lord is close to the brokenhearted; He rescues those who are crushed in spirit."

The sacrifices of God are a broken spirit; a broken and contrite heart O God thou will not despise.

Psalm 51:17

When it comes to repentance, there is contrition or the brokenness of heart referred to as the smiting of the breast (Luke 18:13), the plucking out of hairs (Ezra 9:3), and the watering of the couch with tears (Psalm 6:6). Charles Spurgeon says that repenting will keep us from adding sin to sin. There must be sincere grieving for sin because of its dishonor to God as well as its defilement of the soul for genuine repentance.

The seal of God's pardon is set upon the melting heart. Note again that God requires a broken spirit. The Good News Bible says, "My sacrifice is a humble spirit, O God; you will not reject a humble and repentant heart." The Living Bible has it this way, "It is a broken spirit you want—remorse and penitence. A broken and a contrite heart, O God, you will not ignore." There is no sacrifice as pleasing to God as a broken spirit because of the sight of and the heinousness of sin. Repenting tears of this sort are the joy of God and of angels.

I say unto you, that likewise joy shall be in heaven over one sinner that repented, more than over ninety and nine just persons which need no repentance. Either what woman having ten pieces of silver, if she lose one piece, doth not light a candle, and sweep the house, and seek diligently till she find it. And when she hath found it, she called her friends and her neighbors together, saying, rejoice with me; for I have found the piece which I had lost. Likewise, I say unto you, there is joy in the presence of the angels of God over one sinner that repented.

Luke 15:7-10

Mary brought her tears and ointment to the feet of Jesus (Luke 7:38). Of the two, the tears were more precious to Him because there is sweetness in repenting tears. Weeping days become festival days. Sorrows are turned into joy according to John 16:20. But all humiliation does not end in deep contrition. If sin is only regarded as a failure of duty to oneself or one's neighbors due to natural infirmity, then repentance for wrong-doing will not be accompanied by deep conviction. But if sin is seen to be against God, an infraction of His will, a challenge to His authority, a reflection on His wisdom, a wrong-doing despite His love, then true repentance will be wrung from the soul. Too many are sorry simply because their sin has been discovered. The shame of disclosure hurt their pride. Then, you have others who are disturbed because of the temporal loss that the suffering of sin entails, and that is not repentance. Too few today seem to be moved to contrition by the sight of the vileness of sin or by the fact that it is evil toward a good and Holy God. Sin defiles the soul's glory; it is a plague, a sore; it changes glory into shame, and it must be repented of.

It was very shocking to the Bible class to be told that such unrepented sin has the devil for its father, shame for its companion, and death for its wages.

(Thomas Watson) Without repentance, there is only final damnation. To repent does mean a change of mind, but then it is also a thorough change of the understanding and all that is in the mind so that it includes an illumination of the Holy Spirit; it includes a discovery of iniquity and a hatred of it, without which there can hardly be a genuine repentance. We must not undervalue repentance. It is a blessed grace of the Holy Spirit, and it is absolutely necessary for salvation.

The repentance which is here commanded is the result of faith; it is born at the same time with faith — they are twins, and to say which is the elder-born passes my knowledge. It is a great mystery; faith is before repentance in some of its acts, and repentance before faith in another view of it; the fact being that they come into the soul together.

C. H. Spurgeon

Now, repentance that makes us weep and abhor our past life because of the love of Christ, which has been pardoned, is the right repentance. It was here that another very lengthy discussion evolved from the Bible class on the basis of what they had been hearing all of their lives that once God forgives us, we are to never let it bother us again. It became a heated discussion with one of the deacons of the church, the late Billy Ward, when he was told that when the Holy Spirit brings up some of our past sins for us to reflect on, He was leading us into having a contrite heart. He was seeking to break our spirit so that we would mourn over what we did. Deacon Ward said to the contrary that it was the devil bringing up the past sins and not the Holy Spirit, and he stated that he was not going to let the devil do him like that. I told him that it was not the devil; it was God trying to give him a contrite heart. He argued that once God forgives, He casts it from Him as far as the East is from the West. I told him that this statement is true as far as God is concerned in taking action against us for our sins, but it is not for us to act like we've never done anything wrong to hurt God. The class was told that when the Holy Spirit reminds us, we are to reflect, grieve, and mourn over how we have caused God pain and then let it go with thanking God for the gift of Jesus Christ.

When I can say, "My sin is washed away by Jesus' blood," and then repent because I so sinned as to make it necessary that Christ should die, I am allowing the Holy Spirit to lead me into having a contrite heart. It must be that kind of repentance that looks at his bleeding wounds, and your heart bleeds because you wounded Christ. That broken heart that breaks because Christ was nailed to the cross is the repentance that brings us salvation. Then there is also repentance which makes us avoid present sin because of the love of Jesus, who died for us. This also is saving repentance. If I avoid sin today because I am afraid of being lost if I commit it, I do not have the repentant heart of a child of God. But when I avoid sin and seek to lead a holy life because of

Christ's love for me, because He gave Himself up for me, and because I am not my own but am bought with a price, then this is the work of the Spirit of God.

In a more general sense, repentance means a change of mind or a feeling of remorse or regret for past conduct. True repentance is a godly sorrow for sin, an act of turning around and going in the opposite direction. This type of repentance leads to a fundamental change in a person's relationship with God. A change of mind of being careful will lead one to resolve that in the future, they will live like Jesus and will not live unto the lusts of the flesh. He hath redeemed us, not with corruptible things as silver and gold, but with His own precious blood (1 Peter 1:18-19). This is the repentance that will save us and the repentance that He asks of us.

The nations of the earth must realize that He does not ask for the type of repentance as on Mount Sinai when they did fear and shake because of the thick dark cloud and lightning that came down on the mountain. However, He asks us to weep and wail because of Him; to look on Him whom we have pierced, and to mourn for Him as a man mourned for his only son. He bids us remember that we nailed the Savior to the tree and asks that this argument make us hate the murderous sins which fastened the Savior there and put the Lord of glory to a humiliating and accursed death. This is the only repentance we have to preach. Matthew Henry says that repentance is a daily duty. He that repents every day for the sins of every day, when he comes to die, will have the sins of only one day to repent of. Short reckoning makes long friends.

DAVID'S PLEA OF REPENTANCE

In the Old Testament, the classic case of repentance is that of King David after Prophet Nathan accused him of killing Uriah the Hittite and committing adultery with Uriah's wife, Bathsheba. David's prayer of repentance for this sin is found in Psalm 51. When Nathan the prophet came unto David after David had known Bathsheba, he cried, "Have mercy upon me, O God, according to thy loving-kindness: according to the multitude of thy tender mercies blot out my transgressions." (Psalm 51:1)

This Psalm was not written for private meditation only but for the public service of song, suitable for the loneliness of individuals who needed to repent. When Prophet Nathan came unto David with the divine message, he aroused David's conscience that had become numb to his action, and made him see the greatness of his guilt. David then wrote Psalm 51. While he was indulging his flesh, he had forgotten the practice of singing psalms in worship. When David's spiritual nature was awakened by the realization of his sin, he returned to worship and poured out his repentance with heartfelt tears. No, we cannot excuse David's transgression. However, his story has great lessons in it. He is an example of being led into contriteness by God to have a broken spirit. He was a man of very strong passions, a soldier, and a king. No other king of his time would have felt any regret for having acted as he did. Therefore, he did not have those restraints of custom and association that, when broken through, would render the offense more monstrous. His sins were detestable to the highest degree; they served as a warning to others, and they reflected corruption, whereas guilt was engraved on the heart of the erring King of Israel. As you read this portion of the book concerning the sin of David, you must dwell most upon his penitence and upon the long series of chastisements which rendered the aftermath of his life such a mournful history.

There are two divisions to this Psalm. Note that in the first twelve verses, there are his confessions and plea for forgiveness, and then in the last seven verses, his gratitude. In Psalm 51:1, he says, "Have mercy upon me, O God." Note that he appeals to the mercy of God before he says anything about his sin. David understood that the pardoning of sin was a pure act of mercy. The mercy of God is revealed in scripture.

His mercy is eternal.

But the mercy of the Lord is from everlasting to everlasting on those who fear Him, and His righteousness to children's children.

Psalm 103:17

His mercy is boundless.

For your mercy is great above the heavens, and your truth reaches to the clouds.

Psalm 108:4

The earth, O Lord is full of thy mercy: teach me thy statutes.

Psalm 119:64

His mercy prolongs life.

It is of the Lord's mercies that we are not consumed, because His compassions fail not. They are new every morning: great is thy faithfulness.

Lamentations 3:22-23

His mercy encourages penitence.

So rend your heart, and not your garments; return to the Lord your God, for He is gracious and merciful, slow to anger, and of great kindness; and He relents from doing harm.

Joel 2:13

His mercy is to forgive sin.

Who is a God like unto thee that pardoned iniquity, and passes by the transgression of the remnant of his heritage? He retained not his anger forever, because he delighted in mercy.

Micah 7:18

And His mercy is on those who fear Him from generation to generation.

Luke 1:50

But God, who is rich in mercy, because of His great love with which He loved us.

Ephesians 2:4

His mercy makes salvation possible.

Not by works of righteousness which we have done, but according to his mercy He saved us, by the washing of regeneration, and renewing of the Holy Ghost.

Titus 3:5

The great theologian and masterful preacher Charles Spurgeon gives a thorough explanation of what David meant by "according to thy loving-kindness." He was saying:

Act, O Lord, like thyself; give mercy like thy mercy. Show mercy such as is in agreement with thy grace O thou Great God of heaven whose nature hath no bound; therefore let thy pardoning love be found." What choice words these are, a rare compound of precious things as love and kindness sweetly blended in one loving-kindness. According to the multitudes of thy tender mercies, let thy most loving compassions come to me, and make thou thy pardons such as these would suggest. Reveal all thy gentlest attributes in my case, not only in their essence but in their abundance. Thy acts of

*goodness is without number, and vast is thy grace;
let me be the object of all thy infinite mercy, and
repeat it all in me. Make my one case an epitome
of all thy tender mercies. By every deed of grace
to others I feel encouraged, and I pray thee let
me add another and a yet greater one, in my own
person, to the long list of thy compassions. Blot
out my transgressions. My revolts, my excesses, are
all recorded against me; but, Lord, erase the lines.
Draw a line through the register. Do away with the
record, though now it seems engraved in the rock
forever; many strokes of thy mercy may be needed,
to cut out the deep inscription, but then thou has a
multitude of mercies, and therefore, I beseech thee,
erase my sins.*

Charles Spurgeon, on Psalm 51

*For thou, Lord, art good, and ready to forgive; and
plenteous in mercy unto all them that call upon thee.*

Psalm 86:5

Wash me thoroughly.

Psalm 51:2

For David, it is not enough to blot out the sin; his
person was defiled, and he wanted to be purified. One
of the things I have discovered is that God washes us
through the process of a broken spirit; we should have
a broken and contrite heart mourning over past sins
long enough to deeply regret what we have done and

then shift our thinking to praising God for what He did in sending Jesus Christ for the forgiveness of sin.

I know this to be true because I allowed Him to bring up things I did in the past, and I took time to grieve and mourn over how I hurt Him, hating what I did so much so that I get no joy out of talking about what I used to do like I previously would. God has given me inner peace from the assurance that I am His child.

One of my favorite hymns in the Baptist Standard Hymnal is #27, "Blessed Assurance." David would have God himself cleanse him, for none but God could do it effectively. For David, the washing must be thorough, and it must be repeated; therefore, he cries multiple times to be washed. The careless soul is content with a nominal cleansing, but the truly awakened conscience desires a real and practical washing and that of a most complete and efficient kind.

Wash me thoroughly from mine iniquity.

Psalm 51:1

Something else was revealed to me in teaching this to my Bible class. It was not the punishment that David cried out against, but the sin. Many murderers are more alarmed at the punishment than at the murder which brought them to the punishment. The thief loves the plunder, though he fears the prison. Not so with David. He is sick of sin as sin; his loudest outcries were against his transgression -- not the consequences of it.

And oh, my dear readers, this is one of the things that made him "a man after God's own heart." When we deal with our sins intentionally, God will help us. When we hate what the Lord hates, He will end it to our joy and peace. This is what happened to me because I accepted and was glad that He broke me, and to this day, I am willing to be broken by Him.

Note what the psalmist David says in 51:3, "For I acknowledge my transgressions, and my sin is ever before me." Who was doing that? It certainly was not the devil, for he wants you to remain in your sin and not to be cleansed. To acknowledge our transgressions in agreement with the Holy Spirit is confession, and to have our sin ever before us is conviction that leads to contrition. It was at this point that Deacon Ward was finally convinced. To acknowledge our transgressions is to confess our sins, but to reflect upon our sins with regret authenticates true confession. We are to own our sins with shame and declare them with sorrow; to reckon them up one by one, and to give a particular account of them. It is to spread them before the Lord, as Hezekiah did Rabshakeh's letter (2 Kings 19:14). We must, with full awareness of our unworthiness, implore God's goodness, that He would be as merciful to us as we have transgressed against Him; that He would do it in His free and full forgiveness of them all.

David says, "Against thee, thee only, have I sinned, and done this evil in thy sight: that thou mightest be justified when thou speaks, and be clear when thou judges." (Psalm 51:4). The deadliness of sin lies in its opposition to God. The psalmist David's sense of sin towards others took a backseat to the force of his feeling of sin against God. Though he had sinned against Uriah the Hittite and his wife Bathsheba, nothing is said of him getting it right with them, but only with God. Why do you think that is? Have you ever thought about it? Well, I have, and I think it is because of the mindset of most.

We go out to get it right with our fellowman and think less of getting it right with God. Yes, we have Christ, but that does not eliminate the need for confessing, repenting, and being contrite for our sins. So David declares, "Against thee and thee only have I sinned" (Psalm 51:4). For David, all of his wrong-doing came to a climax at the foot of the divine throne. We violate the law of God when we injure our fellow men in sin, but we are not to focus upon them more than on God. The truly repentant heart is so filled with a sense of the wrong done to the Lord that all other confessions are swallowed up in a broken-hearted acknowledgment of the offense against God. The psalmist David realizes that he had done evil in God's sight. To commit treason in the very court of the king and before His eye is presumption indeed. David felt that his sin was committed in all its filthiness while Jehovah Himself looked on. None but a true child of God cares for the eyes of God. Where there is grace in the soul, it reflects a fearful guilt upon every evil act, and we all need to get there. When we remember that the God whom we offend is present when the trespass is committed, it should cause us to think before we act. It was at this point that I shared with my Bible Class to stop involving the Holy Spirit in their sordid acts because if they are saved, the Holy Spirit is within them, and they can't take Him out and leave Him somewhere until they finish sinning and then go back and get Him. They were to realize that He is there all while they are involved in whatever is displeasing to God. It moved upon the whole class, for they hadn't thought of it that way, and I praise the Holy Spirit for revealing it to me.

David goes on to say, "That thou mightest be justified when thou speaks, and be clear when thou judges" (Psalm 51:4). He could not present any argument against divine justice, even if it proceeded at once to condemn and punish him for his crime. His own confession and the judge's own witness of the whole transaction places the transgression beyond all question or argument; the iniquity was indisputably committed and was unquestionably a sinful act, and therefore the course of justice was clear and beyond all controversy. In verse Psalm 51:5, he says, "Behold, I was shaped in iniquity." He was thunderstruck at the discovery of his inbred sin and proceeded to set it forth.

This was not intended to justify him but rather to complete the confession. It is as if he said that not only had he sinned this once, but that he was in his very nature a sinner. The fountain of his life was polluted, as well as its streams. From birth, he had a tendency toward unrighteousness. He naturally leaned to forbidden things. David was saying that his sins were a constitutional disease, rendering his very person as being obnoxious to God's wrath.

And in sin did my mother conceive me.

Psalm 51:5

He goes back to the earliest moment of his being, not to expose shame or blame by means of falsehood and misrepresentation of his mother, but to acknowledge the deep-tapped roots of his sin. It is wicked to twist the Word of God to deny that the original sin and natural depravity of man is a fact. Surely men who split hairs at this teaching need to be taught, by the Holy Spirit, the first principles of the faith. David's mother was the Lord's handmaid; he was born in chaste wedlock of a good father, and he was himself "a man after God's own heart," and yet his nature was as fallen as that of any other son of Adam, and it only needed the occasion of being tempted for the manifestation of that sad fact.

DAVID'S PRAYER REQUEST AFTER REPENTANCE

Create in me a clean heart, O God; and renew a right spirit within me.

Psalm 51:10

True repentance brings this request from a person. I know this to be true because I personally have asked God to do the same for me. David's request was for God to let His power be seen in a new creation within his old fallen self. He knew that it was God who made man in the beginning, so he cried, "Lord, make a new man in me!" He wanted a clean heart. Therefore he says to God in Psalm 51:7, "Purge me with hyssop, and I shall be clean: wash me, and I shall be whiter than snow." Here, he asked to be cleaned. Further down in verse 10, he seeks a heart clean enough to dwell in his renewed being, but he knows better than to ask God to clean his old heart. David knows that the old nature is hopeless. He wanted God to bury the old man so He could become a new creature. David realized that none but God could create either a new heart or a new earth.

Salvation is a marvelous display of supreme power. The work in us as well as the work for us is the whole of an omnipotent God. The heart (mind) is the rudder of the soul, and until the Lord takes it in His hands, we will steer in a false and sinful way. David's request is, "O Lord, thou who didst once make me, now be pleased to make me new, and in my most secret parts renew me. Renew a right spirit within me. It was there once, Lord; put it back." David knew that the law in his heart had become like an inscription that was hard to read. He pleaded, "Write it now, gracious God. Remove the evil and replace it with good."

I understand why he wanted the evil removed, and I also understand why he wanted something to be put in its place. Though he did not know at that time what Jesus was going to say about having a clean heart in the New Testament.

When an evil spirit comes out of a person, it goes through dry places looking for a place to rest. But it doesn't find any. Then it says, 'I'll go back to the home I left.' When it arrives, it finds the house unoccupied, swept clean, and in order. Then it goes and brings along seven other spirits more evil than itself. They enter and take up permanent residence there. In the end, the condition of that person is worse than it was before. That is what will happen to the evil people of this day.

Matthew 12:43-45

The psalmist David continues in Psalm 51:11, "Cast me not away from thy presence, and take not thy Holy Spirit from me." He was saying, "Throw me not away as worthless; banish me not, like Cain, from thy face and favor. Permit me to sit among those who share thy love, though I may only be a doorkeeper. I deserve to be forever denied admission to thy courts, but, O great and awesome God, permit me still the privilege which is dear as life itself to me." (Charles Spurgeon)

He did not want God to take away His love, guidance, or Spirit. David knew that without those things, he would be a dead man. David did not want God to leave him as He had left Saul. David couldn't imagine a life without the voice and presence of God. He realized that the Spirit of God was his wisdom, so he prayed, "Leave me not to my folly." He acknowledges that God was his strength. Therefore, he asked not to be deserted to his own weakness.

He went on to say to God, "Drive me not away from thee; neither do thou go away from me. Keep up the union between us, which is my only hope of salvation." I can imagine David said within his spirit, "It will be a great wonder if so pure a spirit agrees to stay in so base a heart as mine." But he then says to the Lord, "It is a mystery, but do it for thy mercy's sake." I can say I truly understand David, for I have had to pray the same as is stated in verse twelve.

Restore unto me the joy of thy salvation; and uphold me with thy free spirit.

Psalm 51:12

Salvation he had known and had known it as the Lord's own. He had also felt the joy that arises from being saved in the Lord, but he had lost it for a while, and therefore he longed for it to return. None but God can give back this joy. He can do it, and we can ask Him to do it. He will do it for His own glory and our benefit. This joy comes not first but follows pardon and purity. In this order, it is safe; in any other order, it is vain presumption or idiotic hallucination. He further said, "Uphold me with thy free Spirit." He was conscious of weakness and mindful of having so lately fallen. He seeks to be kept on his feet by a power superior to his own. The Holy Spirit is able to make us walk as kings and priests in all the uprightness of holiness, and He will do so if we seek His gracious upholding. In the best paths, we will stumble if left to ourselves, but in the roughest and most treacherous ways, we are safe with a keeper such as He is. Praying for joy and upholding go well together. It is all over with joy if the foot is not kept; and, on the other hand, joy is a very upholding thing and greatly aids holiness; meanwhile, the Holy Spirit is at the center of both.

Then will I teach transgressors thy ways; and sinners shall be converted unto thee.

Psalm 51:13

It was David's fixed resolve to be a teacher of others, and assuredly none instructs others so well as those who have been experientially taught of God themselves. The pardoned sinner's matter will be good, for he has been taught in the school of experience, and his manner will be telling, for he will speak sympathetically, as one who has felt what he declares. Note the ones that the psalmist David chooses to instruct. He would instruct transgressors like himself; others might despise them, but when we can relate or when we can identify with them, it makes us just like them. The mercy of God toward one is an illustration of his usual procedure so that our own case helps us to understand God's ways or His general modes of action. David refers to the perceptive part of the word of God, which, having broken and having suffered thereby, he felt that he could vindicate and urge upon other offenders like himself.

In Psalm 51:13, David was saying that his fall shall be the restoration of others, that God will bless his pathetic testimony to the recovery of many who, like himself, have turned aside unto crooked ways. Doubtless, this Psalm and the whole story of David have produced for many ages the most beneficial results in the conversion of transgressors, and therefore, evil has been overruled for good. The teaching of the psalmist David continues in verse fourteen.

Deliver me from bloodguiltiness, O God, thou God of my salvation: and my tongue shall sing aloud of thy righteousness.

Psalm 51:14

David had been the means of the death of Uriah the Hittite, a faithful and attached follower, and he now confesses that fact. Besides, his sin of adultery was a capital offense, and he put himself down as one worthy to die. Honest penitents do not look for ways to confess their sins in an elegant speech of many words, but he comes to the point, calling a spade a spade, and makes a clean break of all. What other course is rational in dealing with the Omniscient? "O God, thou God of my salvation." God had not ventured to come so near before. Up until now, David had only cried "O God," but here he cries, "Thou God of my salvation." Faith grows through the exercise of prayer. He confesses sin more plainly in this verse than before, and yet he deals with God more confidently. Growing upward and downward at the same time are perfectly consistent.

It was a challenge to show the Bible Class how one grows upward and downward at the same time, but through the Holy Spirit's guidance, they understood. They were told that growing upward was to always see themselves as one of God's children, adopted into His family as a son or daughter, but to grow downward at the same time was to always see themselves as being unworthy and undeserving. The psalmist David knew that none but the King could remit the death penalty. It is, therefore, a joy to have faith that God is King and that He is the author and finisher of our salvation. Now I see the psalmist committing himself in saying, "And my tongue shall sing aloud of thy righteousness."

One would rather have expected him to say, "I will sing of thy mercy," but David could see the divine way of justification, that is, the righteousness of God which Paul afterward spoke of by which the ungodly are justified, and David vows to sing, yea, and to sing full of strength and vitality of that righteous way of mercy. Note how the psalmist would preach in the last verse, and now here, he would sing. We can never do too much for the Lord, to whom we owe everything. If we could be preachers, pastors, presenters, doorkeepers, ushers, deacons, choir members, and all-in-one, it would all would be too little to show forth all of our gratitude. A great sinner pardoned makes a great singer. Sin has a loud voice, and so should our thankfulness. We shall not sing our own praises if we are saved, but our theme will be the Lord our righteousness, in whose merits we stand righteously accepted. This is the prayer of the penitent psalmist David "O Lord, open thou my lips, and my mouth shall show forth thy praise." He is so afraid of himself that he commits his whole being to the divine care of God and fears to say anything until the Lord unstops his shame-silenced mouth.

This prayer is a golden petition for a preacher. C. H. Spurgeon prayed this prayer for himself and his brethren. How marvelously the Lord can open our lips, and what divine things that we poor sinful believers can pour forth under His inspiration! If God opens the mouth, He is sure to have the fruit of it. According to the porter, at the gate is the nature of that which comes out of a man's lips; when vanity, anger, falsehood, or lust unbar the door, the most offensive words come out; but if the Holy Spirit opens your mouth, then grace, mercy, peace, and all the graces come forth in tuneful dances, like the daughters of Israel when they met David returning with the Philistine's head.

For thou desires not sacrifice; else would I give it: thou delight not in burnt offering.

Psalm 51:16

Verse 16 shows the growth and development of the psalmist. He says, "For thou desire not sacrifices." The reason he can here agree that God would not accept a sacrifice nor be pleased with a burnt offering is because no particular sacrifices were appointed by the Law of Moses to make amends for the guilt of murder and adultery. The person who had perpetrated these crimes was, according to the divine law, to be punished with death. The psalmist David is to be understood as declaring that it was utterly vain for him to think of turning to sacrifices and burnt offerings with a view to the compensation of his guilt, that his criminality was of such a character that the ceremonial law made no provision for his deliverance from the doom which his deeds of horror deserved. The only sacrifices that would avail were those mentioned in previous chapters, "the sacrifice of a broken heart."

This was worth its weight in gold for me and the Bible Class. From this teaching, not only was I personally delivered, but I witnessed the deliverance of many in the church. One, in particular, was the late

Rev. Joseph Mann, one of the associate ministers of the Rehoboth Baptist Church. He was faithful and dedicated to the Lord and to me as his pastor. He was carrying around hatred for some members of his family that was destroying him, but after this teaching on repentance, he became broken and contrite. He wept and mourned over the situation concerning his family. He later came to me and thanked me for the teaching on "David's Prayer of Repentance." He forgave and was set free; he had peace within, and knowing what I know about him, I believe that he is with the Lord.

The understanding of David from verses 16-17 suffers from the perspective of most who say that they are a child of God. David says, "For thou desire not sacrifice, else would I give it: thou delight not in burnt offering?" David wondered what he could give that would be fit to offer to God for all his loving-kindness. He thought upon sacrifices, for they had sometimes been pleasing to God, and He hath oftentimes smelt a sweet odor from them. What does God consider to be a great sacrifice from us today? The sacrifices of God are a broken spirit: a broken and contrite heart, which He will not despise (Psalm 51:17).

Sadly, today, people still do not realize that this is what God is looking for. David makes it clear that the bullocks that are to be sacrificed now are our hearts. He realizes that it was easier for him to give God bullocks for sacrifices than to give God his heart. David meditates with himself and asks himself a question. "Why should I offer Him that for which He does not care? My heart, I know, He cares for; and if it be broken and offered up by penitence and contrition, it is the only sacrifice in which He now delights." Do we think God to be so indifferent that He will accept of us a broken heart? Is a thing that is broken good for anything? Can we drink from a broken glass? Or can we lean upon a broken staff? But though other things may be the worse from being broken, a heart is never at its best until it is broken. Until our heart is broken, we cannot see what is in it. Until it is broken, it cannot send forth its sweetest odor; and therefore, though God loves a whole heart in affection, He loves a broken heart in sacrifice.

Psalm 34:18 says, "The Lord is near to those who have a broken heart." He is near in friendship to accept and console. Broken hearts think God is far away when He is really most near to them; their eyes are blinded so that they see not their best friend. The understanding here is that God is with them and in them, but they don't realize it. They run here and there, seeking peace in their own works, experiences, proposals, and resolutions when the Lord is near them. The simple act of faith will reveal Him, and He will save such as have a contrite spirit. What a blessed token for the good that is a repentant, mourning heart! Just when the sinner condemns himself, the Lord graciously absolves him. If we chasten our own spirits, the Lord will spare us. He never breaks with the rod of judgment those who are already sore with the rod of conviction. Salvation is linked with contrition.

May the reading of this book lead to this reality of saying what Charles Spurgeon mentions in his book, "The Treasury of David," as he notes, "Therefore, accept, O God, my broken heart, which I offer thee with a whole heart."

I place emphasis afresh on what the prophet Isaiah says in Isaiah 66:2, "For all those things my hand has made, and all those things exist," Says the Lord. "But on this one will I look: On him who is poor and of a contrite spirit, and who trembles at my word." God will look with a favorable eye to him that hath a broken and contrite spirit, whose heart is subdued to the will of God, and who is poor and low in his own eyes. He who trembles when he hears God's threatening words and hears every revelation of His will with reverential fear will honor God. I also place emphasis afresh on this scripture, Isaiah 57:15, "For thus saith the high and lofty One that inhabited eternity, whose name is Holy; I dwell in the high and holy place, with him also that is of a contrite and humble spirit, to revive the spirit of the humble, and to revive the heart of the contrite ones." Now this next scripture is wonderful to know.

He healeth the broken in heart, and binds up their wounds.

Psalm 147:3

The Lord is not only a Builder but a Healer. He restores broken hearts as well as broken walls. The kings of the earth think themselves to be great through their loftiness, but Jehovah becomes great by His humility. Behold, the Most High has to do with the sick and the sorrowful, with the wretched and the wounded! He walks the hospitals as the Good Physician! We do not have to send Him because He is already there. The true story is told of a patient that was in the Intensive Care Unit in the hospital. He was lying there praying as though he was alone, but when he finished praying, God answered him immediately through the sign in the room that he was in. The sign was "ICU" (I SEE YOU), and he was made to be calm.

God's deep sympathy with mourners is a special mark of His goodness. Few will associate with the despondent, but Jehovah chooses their company and abides with them until He has healed them by His comforts. He deigns to handle and heal broken hearts. He himself binds up the bleeding wounds of those convinced of sin. There is no compassion like our God.

I pray that all will praise Him to whom He has acted graciously. The Lord is always healing and binding. This is no new work to Him. He has done it of old, and it is not a thing of the past of which He is now weary. Come, broken hearts, come to the Physician who never fails to heal; uncover your wounds to Him who so tenderly binds them up! The psalmist David closes Psalm 51 by making a request to God.

To do good in thy good pleasure unto Zion. Build thou the walls of Jerusalem.

Psalm 51:18

He was saying to God to let blessings according to His pleasure be poured upon His holy hill and chosen city. Zion was David's favorite spot, whereon he had hoped to erect a temple. He felt that he had hindered the project of honoring the Lord there as he desired, but he prayed for God to still let the place of His Ark be glorious and to establish His worship and His worshipping people. Build thou the walls of Jerusalem. It is believed that David had a more spiritual meaning in mind as he prayed for the prosperity of the Lord's cause and people. He had done mischief by his sin, and had, as it were, pulled down her walls. He, therefore, implores the Lord to undo the evil and establish His church. God can make his cause to prosper, and in answer to prayer for Him to do it for His own glory, He will do so. Without His building, we labor in vain; therefore, are we the more instant and constant in prayer? There is surely no grace in us if we do not feel for the church of God and take a lasting interest in its welfare.

Then shall thou be pleased with the sacrifices of righteousness, with burnt offering and whole burnt offering: then shall they offer bullocks upon thine altar.

Psalm 51:19

David is to be understood as saying in those days of joyful prosperity, the people of God would present in great abundance the richest and holiest thank offerings to God, and that God would be pleased to accept them. A saved soul expects to see their prayers answered in a revived church and then is assured that God will be greatly glorified. Though we bring no more sacrifices for sin, as priests unto God, our solemn praises and vowed gifts are thank offerings acceptable to God by Jesus Christ. We bring to the Lord, not our least things (our doves and pigeons), but we present Him with our best possessions (our bullocks of broken hearts). We are glad that in this present time, we are able to fulfill in person what this verse says. We today, forecasting the future, wait for days of the divine presence, when the church of God, with unspeakable joy, shall offer gifts upon the altar of God, which will far eclipse anything beheld in those less enthusiastic days.

THE DYNAMICS OF PRAYING ACCORDING TO THE WILL OF GOD

This is what the Lord has revealed to me when it comes to praying according to His will. It is praying that we may secure an answer according to the promises made in His Word.

And this is the confidence that we have in Him that, if we ask anything according to His will, He heareth us: And if we know that He hears us, whatsoever we ask, we know that we have the petitions that we desired of Him.

1 John 5:14-15

The word "anything" in the verse is usually taken out of context. It is taken to mean anything that my heart desires physically or materially when it is not that at all. Although God does bless us materially, when He does so, He has an ultimate end. Christ is concerned more about our eternal state than our temporal existence. It is not just for anything that we want because we mostly ask for things of the flesh for which the promises in scripture do not apply. Therefore He will not grant the request, making it appear that what He says in His Word is not true. When it comes to prayer, I found out that the promises are true when we properly study the context. The verse says, "according to His will," which is according to what is written in His word concerning your particular situation. One must find a similar situation in scripture where He granted it before and pray accordingly because God's Word is His will for our lives. I have been shown that even after you do the above, it has to be done with the right attitude, meaning that you must not ask Him to do it for you personally but for Himself, and because His Word says so. You must have the attitude of wanting Him to honor His own Word. That has to be the reason for you asking Him to do what you want done; it has to be for Him.

He is always to be primary, and we are secondary. What has been shown to me, and I'm writing it for the benefit of all who read this book, is that we have to understand that God is all about Himself, and He has the right to be that way because He is God, and there is none other.

For of Him, and through Him, and to Him, are all things: to whom be glory forever. Amen.

Romans 11:36

He is all about fulfilling the scriptures. Jesus says

in the gospel of John, John 6:38, "For I came down from heaven not to do mine own will, but the will of Him that sent me." Then in other areas of scripture, you will find:

But all this was done, that the scriptures of the prophets might be fulfilled.

Matthew 26:56

Therefore when it comes to praying according to the will of God, we must find it in scripture where God was asked to do something that only He could do, and He did it upon the request of the person involved. One such incident was when Joshua, the leader of Israel's army, was at war with the Amorites. He asked God to control nature in keeping the sun from going down for about a whole day while they were in battle (Joshua 10:12-13). In Joshua asking God to hold the sun, God stopped it in the sky, and it hastened not to go down for about a whole day. The emphasis is on the fact that God was asked to control nature, and He did.

The story is told of a pastor who asked God to control nature. He prayed according to the will of God. He found his situation in scripture and prayed accordingly, and he received an answer just like Joshua. This particular pastor in previous times had found his situation in the scriptures and prayed, but he asked God to do it for him personally and not to the glory of God, and though he prayed according to the will of God, his prayer was more about himself than it was for God. This pastor's particular situation was that he had a lot of family coming in for a major holiday, and everyone was to have a fellowship at his church. The forecast was for rain in the 70% to 80% range. It was to be a downpour all that weekend. He asked God to control the rain, which would be controlling nature. His reason for making such a request was not just for him and his family but for God. His concern for what they would think about God outweighed what he wanted for himself. The church had some embarrassing water leaks right in the hallway, where they would have to set out containers to catch the water if there had been a downpour.

With all his family coming to the church that Sunday morning, he saw a negative reflection being cast upon God and His house of worship. He cared about what his family and others would think about God. There was a time that it would have been only about him and his embarrassment and not God, but he had grown to care about what would be said about God. He had the attitude of Moses in Exodus 32:10-14, and he cared about God. He found out that when one learns to pray according to the will of God and for His glory, your prayers will be answered. Though the percentage for the chance of rain was high, and there should have been a downpour, he saw God controlling nature as He did for Joshua in the valley. It rained on and off softly all weekend, but it wasn't a downpour. It reminded him that Joshua still had to fight the

Amorites, but God held the sun and kept it from going down until the battle was won. He had worship service that Sunday, and his family was there, and they didn't have to set out containers in the hallway to catch the water. And for that, the pastor was grateful.

This pastor learned another dynamic in praying according to the will of God. His faith was tested during the whole process. He had to stay in meditational prayer with God even while he was enjoying his family. As Joshua had to participate, so he had to participate. Dark moving clouds would form like it was getting ready for a downpour, but the pastor, through the Holy Spirit, never doubted. He kept reinforcing his belief based on the promise made in God's Word. He kept reminding God of the promise He made in His Word that if you ask anything according to His will, He will hear us, and if we know that He hears us, we know that we have the petition that we ask.

One might think that it is wrong or that it is an insult to remind an omniscient, all-knowing God of anything, but God loves it. He wants you to remind Him, not as though He has forgotten, because He hasn't. It is more about you than Him. The more you keep lifting up the promise, the more His Word becomes embedded in you, and that's what God wants. When it comes to the dynamic of praying according to God's will, I gave my congregation an example that if there was sickness, especially a terminal illness, in their lives, they should pray according to the woman with the issue of blood for twelve years.

And a woman having an issue of blood twelve years, which had spent all her living upon physicians, neither could be healed of any, came behind him [Jesus], and touched the border of his garment: and immediately her issue of blood stanched. And Jesus said, 'Who touched me?' When all denied, Peter and they that were with him said, 'Master, the multitude throng thee and press thee, and sayest thou, who touched me?' And Jesus said, 'Somebody hath touched me: for I perceive that virtue is gone out of me.' And when the woman saw that she was not hid, she came trembling, and falling down before him, she declared unto him before all the people for what cause she had touched him, and how she was healed immediately. And he said unto her, 'Daughter, be of good comfort: thy faith hath made thee whole; go in peace.

Luke 8:43-48

She believed that Jesus could heal her, and she pressed her way through the crowd to get to Him. She was healed because of her faith. Only do not make God a last resort as she did. Also, consider the man with the palsy.

And, behold, men brought in a bed a man which was taken with palsy: and they sought means to bring him in, and to lay him before him [Jesus]. And when they could not find by what way they might bring him in because of the multitude, they went upon the housetop and let him down through the tiling with his couch into the midst before Jesus. And when he saw their faith, he said unto him, 'Man, thy sins are forgiven thee.'

Luke 5:18-20

He was healed by the faith of others because the Word of God clearly stated that it happened when Jesus saw their faith.

The information in this book on prayer revolves around the past 30 years of my life. This is what God has revealed to me concerning prayer, and my life has been revolutionized. It is my sincere desire that you will experience the same. I hope this book on understanding prayer will help change your life. I pray that this book blesses all who read it as much as it has blessed me in my experience of writing it. I pray that this book will help lead to a spiritual awakening that will deepen your understanding of prayer and enhance your intimate relationship with God so that your life will be transformed just as mine has been.

APPENDIX

AN EXTRAORDINARY PRAYER

SCRIPTURE REFERENCE 1 Chronicles 4:9-10
DELIVERED June 26, 2016
INTRODUCTION

The Bible has an extraordinary prayer tucked away in the Old or First Testament that was easy for God to answer; it is the "Prayer of Jabez". And Jabez made a prayer to the God of Israel, saying If only you would truly give me a blessing, and make wider the limits of my land, and let your hand be with me, and keep me from evil, so that I may not be troubled by it! And God gave him his desire (1 Chronicle 4:10).

2. It took the Lord over forty-two years of preaching and nearly forty years of being a pastor to bring me to the point of praying out of the ordinary, praying more for spiritual blessings of eternity over against temporal blessings for this life only. In this prayer of Jabez God is going to show us the type of prayers He will grant

immediately. Now this is how we want our prayers to be answered.

3. The Prayer of Jabez is a prayer that was offered up to God long ago and is recorded for our benefit from a spiritual perspective and not material. Things to be noted is that Jabez's achievements are not recorded, though there had to have been many, only his prayer is recorded for our instruction and imitation.

4. This brief but blessed prayer of Jabez is a refreshing spring. What was the nature of his prayer? This child of sorrow prayed for spiritual prosperity, the enlargement of his coast, and deliverance from evil, and his request was readily granted. Jabez showed great spiritual discernment in his praying the way he did. He prayed, not to be kept from evil, but kept from being grieved by evil.

5. While God does not provide temptation, He yet permits it for the strengthening of character. Oh, how we need to make this Old Testament saint's prayer our own! Each of us is in deep need of more honorable blessings, widening horizons of faith, and a more constant liberation from sin's dominion.

6. We all are aware of how this nation is guilty of apostasy, a denial of the faith, and a turning away from God. FIRST, we have **"An Outstanding Man"** This remarkable man named Jabez lived soon after the Israelites took possession of Canaan; and when they were greatly distressed and harassed by the inhabitants

of the land, he showed his spirituality by his earnest desire for the full possession of the promised by seeking it from God through prayer.

7. We know nothing whatsoever of Jabez here commemorated beyond what we find in two verses of the Bible, but this is enough to mark him out as worthy in no ordinary degree of being admired and imitated. There is spiritual depth in the registered prayer of this unknown individual.

8. He was unknown except for his prayer, which should suffice to make him a teacher of the righteous in every generation. Let us now take the several parts of the text in succession, commenting upon each and searching out the lessons which may be useful to us.

9. The first verse contains a short account of Jabez; the second is occupied by his prayer. Now there is no denying that we are short-sighted beings, so little able to look into the future that we are constantly miscalculating as to what would be for our good.

10. We often time anticipate evil from what is working for our benefit, and we look for benefit from that which proves to be burdened with nothing but evil. How frequently does that which we have baptized with our tears make us shine bright with smiles?

11. The tears of oppression of a child of God are known as liquid prayers for David says in Psalms 6:8, thou has heard the voice of my weeping. The word voice in the

Hebrew language denotes the idea of one scratching something across a backboard that creates a squealing noise that irritates the ear of God.

12. How frequently, again, does that which we have welcomed with smiles squeeze from us tears! We do not know the particular reasons which influenced the mother of Jabez to call him by that name, a name which means "sorrowful.

13. We are merely told his mother called his name Jabez, saying, because I bare him with sorrow. His mother having suffered so much during her pregnancy with him, that she called him "Jabez," or Sorrowful, perhaps the time of his birth was the time of her widowhood.

14. Jabez's mother evidently felt but little of a mother's joy and looked on her infant with apprehension and fear. Listen: The way this world has become today is causing many mothers whose children gave them joy at birth and in many instants is bringing them sorrow now.

15. Listen: Whether it was that she brought forth this son with more than common anguish, or whether it was at a time that it was not advantageous to have children, but her sorrow was emphatically turned into joy if she lived to see how excellent a man he turns out to be.

16. Jabez was more honorable than his brethren.

Nothing is told us of his brethren, except that they were less honorable than Jabez; they may have been good men, as is implied, by the word "More", but Jabez took the lead, and whether or not he was the youngest, he surpassed the other in holiness.

17. SECONDLY we have **"An Outstanding Prayer"** His prayer which is here recorded, and which, like Jacob's, in Gen. 28:20), seems to have been uttered when he was entering an important service. Listen, for the successful execution of what was to be done, he placed no confidence in himself or his people's ability.

18. He looked anxiously for the aid and blessing of God. The undertaking was the expulsion of the Canaanites from the territory that was given them by God; and as this was a war of extermination, it was one that God Himself had commanded.

19. His blessing could be more reasonably asked and expected in preserving them from all the evils to which the undertaking might expose him. Jabez enjoyed a remarkable degree of prosperity, and God, in this instance, proved that He was not only the hearer but the answerer of prayer. God granted his request.

20. Now as I have stated Jabez lived soon after Israel took possession of Canaan. Watch this: He prayed as an heir of a temporal Canaan, but ours is a great and more enduring heritage, it is eternal in the heavens with the Lord. Will you pray to receive your heritage?

21. Listen: From a full heart, Jabez earnestly entreats the God of Israel to "bless him indeed!" He didn't want God to bless him like Esau, with temporal blessings. Remember Esau sold his birthright which was his spiritual blessing to Jacob for a bowl of pottage, a bowl of stew.

22. What is the first petition of this earnest child of God at the throne of grace? "Oh," says he, "that Thou would bless me indeed!" Now what sort of blessing does he mean? Life itself is a blessing; health is a blessing; food and raiment is a blessing; so are our friends, and the home that we live in.

23. But it is clearly something beyond these that Jabez asks for. His language is strong: "Oh that Thou would bless me indeed!" He as much as said, "Oh that Thou would give me Thy best, Thy truest blessings!" And what are they? Not the short-lived blessings of the body, but the eternal blessings of the soul.

24. The man is "Blessed Indeed," not as he who sits down to a full table and wears the best of clothes, drives the finest car, and lives in the most emasculate home, but he who can say with a good Scripture guarantee, "Christ is mine and I am His."

25. He is "Blessed Indeed" to whom the God of grace hath said, "I am thy salvation" with whose spirit the Holy Spirit itself bearing witness that you are a child of God" -- and one who is kept by the power of God through faith unto salvation ready to be revealed in

the last time. I have taught my congregation that it is one thing for another to tell you they believe you are a Christian or for you to tell yourself that you are a Christian, but have the Holy Spirit told you that you are a child of God, have you heard from God, has He bore witness to your conversion. We need to do this because others will lie to you and above all you will lie to yourself and that is the worst lie you can tell is to lie to yourself.

26. Other things are blessings; but they are the blessings of Satan, things of the world. Yes: Other things may be considered blessings, but they are temporal and transitory, and they perish with the use, but the choicest gift of God does not perish with the use.

27. Listen: If you want grace to enjoy here and glory hereafter, then be like Jabez. He wanted a spiritual blessing. He was not like Esau's, pottage to satisfy the flesh. Most of the people in the world want pottage, but give me Christ and His Cross, because I'm looking to the hereafter.

28. THIRDLY we have "**An Outstanding Request,**" The text says: And Jabez called on the God of Israel, saying, Oh that thou would bless me indeed, AND enlarge my coast, and that thine hand might be with me, AND that thou would keep me from evil, that it may not grieve me!

29. Christian disciples may use the same prayer; we have to ask that our coast may be enlarged and

that He will keep us from evil. How much are these blessings undervalued, and how little they are realized, and prayer is offered up for God the grant them?

30. How much of the Bible has been unexamined by us? We have our favorite parts, and only give an occasional notice to the rest. How little practical use do we make of God's promises? What need, then, for the prayer, "Oh that Thou would enlarge my coast if I'm not restricting myself to spiritual things? His prayer had to have been spiritual because Israel was not to mix with the inhabitants of the land, but they were to reveal God to them.

31. Now are we only to pray? Are we not also to struggle, for the enlargement of our coasts? Indeed we are: observe how Jabez proceeds, he says, and that Thine hand might be with me." He represents himself as working with God for the enlargement of his coast, but knowing all the while that the battle is the Lord's."

32. Jabez was constrained to fight against the Canaanites; but he conducted the war with faith and prayer, and he entreated the Lord to be with him, both to enlarge his coast and to preserve him front disastrous events, that would tear him down rather than build his faith.

33. In the land of Canaan ancient believers saw a type of heaven; in their wars with the Canaanites, it represented the conflict of God's people with their enemies. Therefore every clause of his prayer may be

applied to, and probably was intended for more noble and spiritual blessings.

34. He wanted to be a blessing to God. And the Lord heard and granted his requests, and therefore he became honorable, as well as prosperous, in Israel. He was prosperous by the way in which he was seen as a scribe who taught many in the way of the Lord.

35. If I have learned one thing in the preaching of the gospel, it is that we must remind the people of the death, burial, resurrection, ascension, and return of the Lord Jesus Christ, which is the gospel, the good news. They need reminding because Satan will do all he can for us to forget that, plus we are invested in a weakness called forgetfulness. Therefore let me tell you that it was late on a Thursday night, they arrested my Lord, led Him away to a kangaroo court...Etc. And on that Friday they crucified Him out on a hill called Calvary. He died when He got ready, no man took His life He laid it down, and they took Him and laid Him in Joseph's new tomb. He stayed there three days and three nights, but early that Sunday morning He rose and step out on resurrection ground and declared that all power in heaven and earth is in my hand. He ascended back to the Father and presented Himself to the Father Holy on our behalf. He return to earth showed Himself to His disciples and hung around for 40 days, being seen by 5000 all at once. Then He boarded a cloud and went back up to heaven while the people stood gazing,

and the angels said to them why to stand here gazing for the same way you see Him going he is coming back again.

BARRIERS TO ANSWERED PRAYER SERMON #1

SCRIPTURE REFERENCE Zechariah 7: 11-13
DELIVERED October 16, 2016
INTRODUCTION

My brother and sisters, if there ever was a means given and demonstrated by our Lord for our benefit, it was that of prayer. Luke 18:1 from the Message translation says: Jesus told them a story showing that it was necessary for them to pray consistently and never quit.

2. We are focusing on the ministry of the ushers this month. If this ministry or any other ministry in this church or any other church is going to serve The Lord effectively, it is going to take those who are in the particular ministry praying. Prayer is a basic need for all God's work.

3. Therefore we need to know what will bar our prayers from being heard and answered. We need to know what it is that is a stumbling block, an obstacle,

a hindrance, a deterrent, a hurdle that our prayers have to clear before God will hear and answer.

4. Israel was a people of God's choice. They were a nation He used to reveal Himself to other nations. Paul knew this would benefit us, he says in Romans 15:4: For whatsoever things were written beforehand was written for our learning that we through patience and comfort of the scripture might have hope.

5. Israel had the wrong understanding of God, they did a lot of assuming with God and it's pretty much the same today when it comes down to God in the area of what He wants. We go on assumptions rather than facts. Saul the first king of Israel made that mistake in his partial obedience in 1 Samuel chapter 15. It cost him the kingdom. It is dangerous to assume on God when He has told you what He wants. Read it at your leisure.

6. Israel had an inadequate view of things that became a strong barrier to their prayers being answered. They had an inadequate view of prayer and God's will. Are there requirements to be met by us before God will answer our prayers, of course, there are...2 Chronicle 7:14. There are four requirements. If my people, which are called by my name, shall (1) humble themselves, and (2) pray, and (3) seek my face, and (4) turn from their wicked ways; then will I hear from heaven, and will forgive their sin, and will heal their land.

7. FIRST we have "**The Prophet Zechariah**

Observation". He observes and gives us a link between prayer and the preach Word of God. It says your ancestors would not listen to my messages when I spoke to them through the prophets.

8. They turned stubbornly away and put their fingers in their ears to keep from hearing. They made their hearts (minds) as hard as stone, so they could not hear the law or the messages that the Lord Almighty had sent them by His Spirit through the earlier prophets. Now I don't foresee them literally putting their fingers in their ears while the prophet was preaching, but God knew they weren't paying attention, their minds were somewhere else while their bodies were sitting there in the congregation. It is one mind that does the hearing and not the two ears on the side of one's head. The scripture says God monitors every thought we have, and with their minds somewhere else was the same as sticking their fingers in their ears.

9. That made the Lord Almighty angry with them. He responded, and since they refused to listen when I called to them, I would not listen when they called to me, says the Lord Almighty. These are Strong words that He will uphold because He says: Heaven and earth will pass away before one jot or one tittle of my word shall fail.

10. Listen to Heb 10:31: It is a fearful thing to fall into the hands of the living God. To fall into the hands of God is to fall under His displeasure, and He who lives

forever can punish forever. How dreadful to have the displeasure of an eternal, Almighty God resting on the soul forever!

11. Zechariah explained to the people what brought the great wrath of God down on them by hardening their hearts to the messages He sends. Do it once and it becomes more natural to do the second time, as we become hardened, each repetition becomes easier.

12. Listen: Ignoring or refusing God's warning will harden you every time in the process of doing wrong. Read God's Word and apply it to your life. Sensitivity and submission to God's Word will soften your heart and allow you to live, as you should.

13. SECONDLY: we have "**Prayer and the Will of God**" The purpose of prayer, reading God's word, and coming to teaching is to discover God's will. Now in order for prayer to be effective it must go hand in hand with the Word of God. I John 5:14 says if we ask anything according to His will He hears us.

14. The will of God is the Word of God. The emphasis here is on God's will and not our will. When we communicate with God, we don't demand what we want; rather we discuss with Him what He wants for us. You and God talk it over so He can show you what is best for you. You and God can't talk it over if you are always preoccupied with other things on your mind other than Him.

15. Listen: When we align our prayers to His will, He will listen; and we can be certain that if He listens, He will give us a definite answer. When it comes to being a good servant for Christ pray according to Luke 17:7-10. Ask the Lord to help you be that servant. I have already given you four sermons on that text. If you don't remember get the CD and replay it. You remember that servant can in from the fields, working all day and before he could do anything for himself he had to take care of his master's needs and he didn't even tell him thank you because it was his duty.

16. The root of Israel's problem was their ignorance of the will of God. The people didn't realize that God's will involves five characteristics. (1) What should be done (2) Who should do it (3) How it should be done (4) Why it should be done, and (5) When it should be done.

17. Listen: If God didn't follow through with those five characteristics of His will. It would just be a thought on His part and the rest is left up to us. God does not leave it up to us, for wherever His will is concerned He directs it all the way.

18. It was God's will that they go into the promised land. He promised Abraham that He was going to give them the land. God keeps His promises. I personally love that about God. He is the only one that can promise, you hear peoples say a lot of times I promise, that making yourself be as God, only He can promise

because only He is not affected by anything that will hinder Him from doing what He says. Things can come up in our lives and we have back down on what we promise. God sent them a message for them to go in and take the land. That was the (What) should be done.

19. You will be led by Joshua (Who) You will possess the land by my power (How) For my glory (Why) God said to them I don't want you to wait, but go in immediately and conquer the land relying on my guidance and power (When) of God message to them.

20. The people turn a deaf ear to Him, they wouldn't follow God's instruction; they ignored His messages and follow their own plan. While they wanted to enter the promised land, they wanted to do it their way and in their time. When we do this we miss out on what God has for us.

21. Don't play around with the messages God sends by His Spirit through the preacher. The Lord hates presumption, false confidence, and self-will. Israel presumed that even though they didn't heed His messages sent through the prophets. God would still help them conquer the land, but they were wrong.

22. THIRDLY and I bid you good morning. We have "**God Response**" Israel had rejected God's word and disobeyed His commands, therefore the Lord would not respond to their prayers. Zechariah says they made their hearts as adamant stones (Very hard) lest they

should hear the law and the words, which He had sent in His Spirit by the prophet.

23. Note what God is saying here. He is not stuttering, He is very clear in our text. God is saying this because you will not hear the man of God when he preaches or proclaims my Words to you. I will not hear you when you cry unto me, and we all know how we cry unto God, it is through prayer.

24. These verses have grave implications for us today. God treats us the way we treat listening to the preached Word of God. The messages He sends. My brother and sisters do you realize this, if you haven't, then allow it to fall fresh on you as to what this is saying. How we listen to sermons is important.

25. Hebrews 2:1 issues a warning, it says: Therefore we ought to give the more earnest heed to the things we have heard lest at any time we let them slip or leak out of our minds. You see familiarity bread contempt, which is having a lack of respect or reverence for something.

26. Listen: One needs to guard against contempt, whether it is familiarity or some other dislike that may crowd your mind, perhaps you have a problem with the preacher/pastor. Deal with it because at some point you are going to need God and you want Him to hear you when you call.

27. The prophet Zechariah is letting us know that

refusing to listen to preaching concerns God greatly. Don't allow a prerogative of God to be meaningless to you. God says in Romans 10: How can they hear without a preacher and how can they preach unless they be sent?

28. Therefore we must listen to messages sent from God. THEN the lord will not turn a deaf ear to our prayers for help. I hear you saying this can't be because He is merciful and we are under grace, that true, but do you understand what mercy is? It keeps God from giving you what you deserve.

29. For grace is the unmerited favor of God whereas He just let you float along, but you could have it so much better if you only obeyed him. So when He let you keep living and you are being rebellious, you are getting mercy. He is giving you a chance to repent and turn.

30. My brother and sisters we need to understand what turning a deaf ear to the messages that God sends have on our prayers being heard. You just don't approach God just any kind of way and He will hear and answer your prayer. Comply or miss your answer.

31. Well one Friday they crucified Him out on a hill called Calvary. He died when He got ready, no man took His life He laid it down, and they took Him and laid Him in Joseph's new tomb. He stayed there three days and three nights, but early that Sunday morning He rose and step out on resurrection ground and

declared that all power in heaven and earth is in my hand. He ascended back to the Father and presented Himself to the Father Holy on our behalf. He return to earth showed Himself to His disciples and hung around for 40 days, being seen by 5000 all at once. Then He boarded a cloud and went back up to heaven while the people stood gazing, and the angels said to them why to stand here gazing for the same way you see Him going he is coming back again.

BARRIERS TO ANSWERED PRAYER SERMON #2

SCRIPTURE REFERENCE Deuteronomy 1:42- 45
DELIVERED October 23, 2016
INTRODUCTION

The Lord revealed to us last Sunday that failing to listen to the messages that He sends by His Spirit through His preacher is a barrier to answered prayer. We were shown that you can have a deficient, ineffective view of prayer and the Will of God.

2. The SECOND barrier to answered prayer is **PRESUMPTUOUS praying**. Presumptuous praying is praying with an attitude or beliefs dictated by probability, knowing that you haven't removed the barrier, but go on and pray making yourself believe He is going to answer.

3. Presumptuous praying is praying on the assumption that God is love and is so full of grace and mercy that He just going to ignore our actions. We must

never presume upon the grace of God to the point of one disobedient and expect God to overlook our disobedience.

4. Nor should we assume that because we've confessed our sins we will not experience any discipline from God. Hebrews 12 says for whom the Lord loves He corrects every child of His. God willingly forgives us but He supports all principles of His Word.

5. Read the 12th chapter of Hebrews in its entirety. It is interesting to know how the heavenly Father loves His children as a good parent. We are to accept correction from Him more so than we accept it from our earthly parents. One thing He makes very clear is that if you be without chastisement you are not one of His children. If God leaves you alone in your wrong He is sending you a very important message, you have been deceived, and you are not His child.

6. FIRST we have "**Israel's Consequences**" The whole context from which the message comes this morning is centered around Moses speaking to the Israelites at the end of the forty years in the wilderness. Now let's understand what brought on the forty years in the wilderness. God had brought them out of Egypt with a mighty hand through His servant Moses. He guided them with the pillow of a cloud that would shade them through the day and light up at night so that they could keep traveling to the promised land. When they got to the Red Sea and Pharaoh's army was coming on

strong, the pillow of cloud went from before them and became a pillow of fire protecting them, then He parted the Red Sea and they went across on dry ground. They had seen Him do too much to doubt Him. Read the Exodus, it is a good read.

7. In our text word we see the Israelites praying to the Lord confessing their sins and yet God refused to listen to their prayers. He would not restore them to their previous position with Him. He ignored the voice of their weeping. David says in Psalms 6:8: Thou hath heard the voice of my weeping. Israel wept before the Lord, but He would not hear their liquid prayers.

8. Listen: He had already given them the promised land and wanted them to possess it. Why didn't God give them success when they decided to go in on their own? God did not answer their prayers and allow them to be successful because He knew they had not weighed their own action against Him. As far as they were concerned what they did was nothing.

9. He knew that their view of spiritual matters was completely unacceptable. They had hurt Him, grieve Him, out of all they had seen Him do, yet they were afraid and doubted. They had not considered nor given any thought to what they had done to God. That is a major problem with us; we don't have the right perception of sin. God hates sin and we think nothing of it.

10. Therefore Moses says in verse 45 "And you returned

and wept before the Lord", but the Lord would not hearken to your voices nor give ear unto you. God is not like a lot of us make Him out to be, which is soft and so understanding so full of love by our definition of love. God's definition of love is not like ours. His is "Agape" meaning He doesn't do for us what we want but what we need. He is a god of love, but only agape style.

11. SECONDLY we have **"Israel's Blindness"** Let's look at some of the spiritual matters and notice how the people failed to understand them. NOTE: The Israelites had confessed their sin yet God did not hear their plea. God did not answer their prayer or allow them to be successful. Why?

12. Israel, like many of us, didn't take sin seriously, they looked upon it lightly. While they said, "We have sinned" their heart was not in their confession. Merely admitting their guilt did not make them truly repentant, there was no remorse, no brokenness, and no contrition. (Isaiah 66: 2) For all those things hath mine hand made, and all those things have been, saith the LORD: but to this man will I look, even to him that is poor and of a contrite spirit, and trembleth at my word.

13. We find a number of examples in the Bible of people who made confession, but did not mean it, who did not tremble at His word. Pharaoh said I have sinned when God was sending the plaques on Egypt, but he

did not mean it as though God didn't know his heart. We think God sees as we see.

14. When God sent the prophet Nathan to confront David about his sin with Bathsheba and the killing of her husband Uriah. David said I have sinned against the Lord and he meant it for he did truly repentant, he was broken and saw the sin as being against God. He said against thee and thee only have I sinned, and done this evil in thy sight.

15. When the Prodigal Son returned home. He also said I have sinned and meant it. In each case, the Lord examined the motives and attitudes and based His response on their seriousness and not just their words. He knows the difference. Israel's motive was to get into the promised land and not have to go back into the wilderness, not because they sin against God.

16. THIRDLY and I bid you good morning. We have "Israel Heart Attitude" All while the children of Israel were saying we have sinned against the Lord their minds were plotting what they were going to do next. What they said and did immediately after said that they were not truly repentant. They loosely thought it out "We have sinned".

17. Listen: Right after almost in the same breath they said we will go up and fight. The Lord had told them through Moses. Do not attempt to conquer the land because He was not with them. Have you ever done that, you have messed up, but....ETC.

18. Their self-will attitude had made them stubborn, they were determined to do it anyway, but they were defeated. Then they return and cry out to God. The text says: And ye returned and wept before the LORD; but the LORD would not hearken to your voice, nor give ear unto you.

19. When we don't have the right attitude, and we have a sarcastic understanding of sin, our prayers are hindered because God has to take time to show us our sins so that we will truly repent and be cleansed. He is out to clean us and not stack sin upon sin.

20. What were the Israelite sins? They had committed the sin of unbelief after God had shown them what He could do. This sin led to another sin the sin of disobedience; they refused to go into Canaan.

21. Then they were guilty of murmuring they complained let's go back to Egypt. God had delivered them so that they could represent Him in the land that He was giving them, but they were afraid to trust God to be with them in the future as He had in the past.

22. Their sins cause them to despair which led to presumption; they said we are sorry for what we have done, but when the consequence for their action was handed down from God. They said we will go up and take the land as God told us at first. They had no idea of the gravity of their sin.

23. They thought they could just tell God we are

sorry and that would be the end of it. It is as far as forgiveness is concerned if you are sincere, but then there are the consequences to deal with. Consequences, Oh consequences, they are a monster…Etc.

24. The Israelites had robbed God of His glory and had disobeyed His expressed will. Therefore He would not listen to their prayers. Like the Israelites, we often don't see sin for what it really is. If we understood how serious are the sins of unbelief, we would flee from that attitude.

25. Well one Friday they crucified Him out on a hill called Calvary. He died when He got ready, no man took His life He laid it down, and they took Him and laid Him in Joseph's new tomb. He stayed there three days and three nights, but early that Sunday morning He rose and step out on resurrection ground and declared that all power in heaven and earth is in my hand. He ascended back to the Father and presented Himself to the Father Holy on our behalf. He return to earth showed Himself to His disciples and hung around for 40 days, being seen by 5000 all at once. Then He boarded a cloud and went back up to heaven while the people stood gazing, and the angels said to them why stand here gazing for the same way you see Him going he is coming back again.

BARRIERS TO ANSWERED PRAYER SERMON #3

SCRIPTURE REFERENCE Psalm 66:18-20
DELIVERED October 30, 2016
INTRODUCTION

My brother and sisters, if there ever was a spiritual exercise that we as Christian disciples need to understand how it works, it is that of prayer. The disciples witness Jesus using it and how God the Father responded to it until they asked, "Master, teach us how to pray."

2. We have been shown that failing to listen to the messages that the Lord sends by His Spirit through His preacher/prophets is a barrier to answered prayer. God says in His word, "Because you would not listen when I call unto you, I will not listen when you call unto me."

3. We were shown a second barrier to answered prayer,

which is presumptuously praying. That is praying with an attitude or beliefs dictated by probability, knowing that you haven't removed the barrier, but go on and pray, saying to ourselves, "He brought me too far to leave me now." It is not that God leaves us, but we leave Him...Etc.

4. This brings us to the "Third Barrier" to answered prayer which is Psalm 66:18: If I regard iniquity in my heart the Lord will not hear me. Another translation says: If I had not confessed the sin in my heart, my Lord would not have listened.

5. Listen: Our confession of sin must be continual because we continue to do wrong, we all have the problem that Paul spoke of in his letter to the Corinthians about when I would do good evil is present with me. Paul wrestles with what I shouldn't do that I find myself doing and what I should do that I don't do. He concluded is saying Oh wretched man that I'm. True confession requires us to listen to God and to want to stop doing what is wrong. David confessed his sin and prayed, "Cleanse me from these hidden faults. Keep me from deliberate sins".

6. I have heard people say I've been praying about something for a long time, and He hadn't answered me. There is a reason He hasn't answered. He doesn't want you to be like the Israelites, they assume that confessing their sins AFTER they saw what the consequences were was sufficient for God, but it was not.

7. FIRST we have "**The Brokenhearted**" Note Psalm 34:18: The Lord is close to the brokenhearted; He rescues those who are crushed in spirit. We often wish we could escape the pain of regret. We do not like to reflect upon our sins.

8. Maybe we need to take time and do some regretting and rightly evaluate what may be happening in our lives. Most of the time we woefully reflect upon our sins, we do it with delight, wishing we could do it again when it ought to be done with regret, groaning in our spirit over you once having done such ungodly things against God.

9. God wants to fulfill His promises to us. He promises to be close to the brokenhearted. Israel's hearts were not broken and their spirit was not crushed, they had not considered nor given any thought to what they had done, and He knows when it is the same with us. Consider those who commit a crime and are incarcerated, while in prison they read the Bible from cover to cover, and make all kinds of promises to God as to how they are going to go to church and serve when they get out. They may come a few Sundays and you don't see them anymore. Their hearts were never broken over whatever it was they had done.

10. Listen to Psalms 51:17: The sacrifices of God are a broken spirit: a broken and a contrite heart, O God, thou wilt not despise. The sacrifice of God is for you to be broken over the sin committed. Knowing that God

hates sin, we should hate it to the point of deep regret and be broken in spirit.

11. All sacrifices are presented to those whose broken heart brings forth the Savior's merit upon their falling into sin. When the heart mourns for sin, God is more pleased than when the bullock was bleeding beneath the axe. Before Christ became our sacrifice many animals died to appease God.

12. SECONDLY we have "**Graceful Mourning.**" Oh how excellent is a spirit humbled and mourning for sin, that it is not only a sacrifice, but it has a plurality of excellences, and it is preeminently God's sacrifices.

13. The Lord is near the brokenhearted; He is the Savior of those whose spirits are crushed down. A heart crushed is a fragrant heart. It sends up a sweet odor in God's nostrils. Men scorn those who are despicable in their own eyes.

14. Oh but the Lord seeth not as man seeth. He despises what men esteem, and values that which they despise. Never yet has God slighted a lowly, weeping penitent heart, and never will He while Christ is continually presenting Himself before the Father.

15. While Jesus is called the man who receives sinners. Bullocks and rams He desires not, but a contrite hearts He seeks after; but only one of them is better to Him than all the rest offered in the old Jewish sanctuary, which is being broken over our sins.

16. Listen: One might expect a joyful rejoicing heart when it comes to being thankful for what God does in our lives, but instead of that he wants a broken and contrite heart. For the joy of forgiveness does not banish sorrow and contrition for sin. It should produce brokenness rather than joyfulness.

17. The deeper the sense of sin, and the truer the sorrow for sin, the more heartfelt also will be the thankfulness for pardon and reconciliation. The tender, humble, broken heart is therefore the best thankful offering that one can give God. But that is not what is being given, largely because we haven't been taught what he wants. We bend over backward to serve, and some work themselves, using one of our idioms, to death in the church, going the extra mile, wanting that to please God, but it doesn't the sacrifice He wants is a broken and contrite heart.

18. I hear you saying what if we are not aware of sins we have committed in our lives. If you are saved you will know whether or not you have committed sin in your life, because the Holy Spirit is in you and that is one of the roles He plays in our lives.

19. THIRDLY we have "The Blessed Holy Spirit" Note what Jesus told His disciples in John 16:7-8: Nevertheless, I tell you the truth. It is to your advantage that I go away; for if I do not go away, the Helper will not come to you; but if I depart, I will send Him to you. And when He has come, He will convict the world of

sin, and of righteousness, and of judgment.

20. Listen: If I'm aware of some sin in my heart and won't acknowledge it then God will not hear me when I pray. Now that is hard for many to accept because we believe our sins are forgiven whether we confess them or not.

21. Listen: The Three important tasks of the Holy Spirit are: (1) Convincing the world of its sin and calling it to repentance. (2) Revealing the standards of God's righteousness to everyone that believes, and (3) To demonstrate Christ's judgment over Satan.

22. Every child of God needs to memorize Proverb 28:13, which says, he that covered his sin shall not prosper, but he that confesses and forsake shall have mercy. The reasons God will not hear or answer our prayers when there is un-confessed sin in our lives in obvious.

23. We wouldn't learn anything from our mistakes. It's human nature to hide our sins or overlook our mistakes. But it's hard to learn from a mistake that we won't acknowledge making. And what good is a mistake if it doesn't teach us something?

24. To learn from an error one has to admit it, confess it, analyze it, and make adjustments so that it doesn't happen again. Everybody makes mistakes, but only fools repeat them.

25. Then my brother and sisters, we have allowed the

devil to hide this from us. If God goes on and answers our prayers over known un-confessed sins. He would be Harding our hearts in sin and encouraging hypocrisy and God will not encourage hypocrisy. He hates the hypocrite.

26. Watch This: Job talks about hypocrisy and prayer in Job 27: 8-9: For what is the hope of the hypocrite though he has gained, but will God hear his cry, [his prayers] when troubles come upon him. Oh, my brothers and sisters we can't afford God turning a deaf ear to our cry.

27. Many people today are so busy trying to accumulate material wealth that they ignore God and how they should be dealing with their sins, but when calamities strike in the storm of life or when sickness comes, we call to God, and wonder why He doesn't answer.

28. We forget that when we regard or cherish a known sin in our lives the Lord will not hear or answer our prayers. To cherish a sin means to practice it secretly, to enjoy a sinful act when you know God is looking upon it with disgust.

29. We must not allow sin to remain in our lives in this manner. We must deal with sin quickly and drastically. Romans 12: 9 says: Let love be without dissimulation. Abhor that which is evil; cleave to that which is good. Be kindly affectionate one to another with brotherly love; in honor preferring one another.

30. I like the way the Psalms ends: The Psalmist says in verses 19 & 20, but verily God has heard me He has attended to the voice of my prayer. Another translation says, but God did listen! He paid attention to my prayer.

31. Praise God, who did not ignore David's prayer and did not withdraw His unfailing love from him all because he stopped regarding iniquity in his heart after Nathan came to him. He confessed, repented, and mourned over his sin says: Against thee and thee only have I sin and have done this great evil in thy sight.

32. Well one Friday they crucified Him out on a hill called Calvary. He died when He got ready, no man took His life He laid it down, and they took Him and laid Him in Joseph's new tomb. He stayed there three days and three nights, but early that Sunday morning He rose and step out on resurrection ground and declared that all power in heaven and earth is in my hand. He ascended back to the Father and presented Himself to the Father Holy on our behalf. He return to earth showed Himself to His disciples and hung around for 40 days, being seen by 5000 all at once. Then He boarded a cloud and went back up to heaven while the people stood gazing, and the angels said to them why stand here gazing for the same way you see Him going he is coming back again.

BARRIERS TO ANSWERED PRAYER SERMON #4

SCRIPTURE REFERENCE Proverb 28:9
DELIVERED November 15, 2016
INTRODUCTION

In our last stand, the Lord revealed to us the "Third Barrier" to answered prayer which is Psalm 66:18: If I regard iniquity in my heart the Lord will not hear me. Iniquity since it has such grave implications barring our prayers from being heard. What is it?

2. Iniquity is being bent or crooked, giving in to treachery, dishonesty, wrongdoing as a breach of trust, and dealing deceitfully. We have an idiom that describes it that was used back in the day call throwing a rock and hiding your hand….Etc.

3. Maybe you are about to give up on something you have been praying for, for a long time, and you are beginning to think God is not going to answer. There

is a reason He hasn't answered. You may be ignorantly making your prayer an abomination to Him through what is stated in Proverbs 28:9.

4. This is the 4th Barrier to Answered Prayer. He that turneth away his ear from hearing the law, even his prayer shall be an abomination. Listen to the Bible in Basic English: As for the man whose ear is turned away from hearing the law, even his prayer is disgusting.

5. FIRST we have **"The Wisdom of Proverbs"** Many of the Proverbs are short sentences, which contain their whole design within themselves and are not connected to one another. The reason being it was a plain and effective way for Solomon to teach so the people could retain.

6. Proverbs carries both sense and evidence in a little compass. They are quickly apprehended and easy to remember. It was a very profitable way of teaching the people to be wise, and it served admirably well as an answer to an end.

7. When you do a word study on Proverb 28:9: He that turns away his ear from hearing, hearing in the Hebrew language means to give undivided listening attention. It is to lend an ear to listening as that of an eavesdropper.

8. The phrase "Even his prayer", prayer in the verse means prayer of intercession for someone else and your own supplication which are specific requests in what

you want God to do for you personally. My brothers and sisters we can't afford not to listen today....Etc.

9. The word abomination in the verse means that which is morally disgusting repugnant, or nauseating to God. You don't want your prayer to make God sick. You want your prayer to move upon Him. It is important to God in no uncertain terms that you don't turn away your ear from hearing His word.

10. Listen to His plea in Proverb 1:22: How long, ye simple ones, will ye love simplicity? And the scorners delight in their scorning, and fools hate knowledge? How long will you go on being simple-minded? How long will you mockers enjoy your mocking? How long will you fools fight the facts?

11. The simple ones are not fools, nor are they someone with a mental deficiency but someone with a character deficiency (such as rebellion, laziness, or anger). The fool is not someone stupid, but he or she is unable to tell right from wrong or good from bad.

12. SECONDLY we have "**The Rebuke of Love**," God says to His peoples: Turn you at my reproof, my rebuke: Behold, I will pour out my spirit unto you, I will make known my words unto you. Turn back to Me at my sharp words: See, I will send the flow of my spirit on you, and make My words clear to you.

13. Pride is thinking more highly of our own wisdom and desires than of God's. To receive His advice, we

must be willing to listen, refusing to let pride stand in our way. If we think we know better than God or feel we have no need for God's direction, we have fallen into foolish and disastrous pride.

14. God says I called to you often, but you didn't come. I reached out to you, but you paid no attention. You ignored my advice and rejected my correction. Therefore I will laugh when you are in trouble! When disaster overtakes you when calamity overcomes you like a storm.

15. God says: I will laugh when anguish and distress overwhelm you. I will not answer when they cry for help. Even though they anxiously search for me, they will not find me for they HATED knowledge and chose not to fear the Lord. It is all in Proverbs 1:26-33, read it in your leisure.

16. Listen to God: They rejected my advice and paid no attention when I corrected them. He let the Israelites go on blindly, stubbornly, and selfishly, when they should have been obeying and following His desires. Look at what made their prayers an abomination, they HATED knowledge.

17. Perhaps you are one of those church members that will come to church right before the preacher gets up to preach. You never come to Sunday school or Wednesday night Bible study, and don't even think of you attending a special seminar on a specific biblical topic.

18. God sometimes lets us continue in our stubbornness to bring us to our senses. He does not keep us from rebelling because He wants us to learn the consequences of sin. He uses these experiences to turn people away from greater sin to faith in Him.

19. The (L.A.B) Life Application Bible has it this way: That is why they must eat the bitter fruit of living their own way. They must experience the full terror of the path they have chosen. For they are simply one's who turn away from me to death.

20. God says they are fools, and their own complacency will destroy them. Many proverbs point out that the fact of the "Bitter Fruit of Living Their Own Way" That is thinking you know better than God by the path you have chosen for your life.

21. Listen: We all are faced with either choosing God's wisdom for our lives or persisting in a rebellious independence. There are so many who decide to go it alone. The problems such people create for themselves will destroy them.

22. Listen: Psalms 9:17: The wicked shall be turned into hell and all the nations that forget God. How solemn is Psalms 9:17, especially in its warning to forgetters of God, and the honest who are not prayerful, the benevolent who do not believe. America is one of those nations.

23. Don't ignore God's advice even if it is painful

for the present. It will yield the peaceable fruit of righteousness to them if it is exercised thereby. God says, but all who listen to Me will live in peace and safety, unafraid of harm. There is a safe haven called "Goshen". This is why I'm not worried about my protection no matter how bad this world gets. I hate the way things are because I filled God's pain, and I'm able to identify with Him. But in the Book of Exodus when God was sending the plagues to Egypt because Pharaoh wouldn't let His people go. One of the plagues was lice that came upon all the Egyptian animals and they were dying, but God's people were doing well over in the land of Goshen. They heard about it so one of the Pharaohs' priest check it out, he goes and look over into the land of Goshen, and true enough all was doing well, there was no disease animals, or anything. He comes back and tells Pharaoh that it's true. Therefore let what comes on America for her gross immorality, when God Judge this nation, I'm one of His children, and I believe I will be put in a modern-day land of Goshen.

24. THIRDLY and I bid you good morning. We have "**The Solution,**" Psalms 1 says blessed in the man who walks not in the council of the ungodly. Nor stand in the path of sinners. Nor sit in the seat of the scornful. This psalm gives the joys of obeying God and refusing to listen to those who discredit or ridicule Him.

25. One's friends and associates can have a profound

influence on us, often in very subtle ways. If we insist on friendships with those who mock what God considers important, we will be tempted and fall into becoming indifferent to God's will.

26. This attitude is the same as mocking. A question for all of us to ask ourselves. Do my friends build up my faith, or do they tear it down? True friends should help you draw closer to God, and not be one that put distance between you and the things of God.

27. The story is told of a young man who grew up in the country and toward the period of moving into his adolescent and teenage years he moves into the city. During his country days, he was taught to go to church and be a part of Sunday school. But when he moved into the city a new peer group became his schoolmates, playmates. His new friends were different from his country friends. One particular Sunday morning his new peer group did not go to church and they persuaded him to go horseback riding...Etc. Peer groups can be persuasive, he found himself yielding to his peer group, and he found himself riding his horse on Sunday morning. Strangely enough, they went through town and pass right by the church at the Sunday school hour with the church bell ringing, His conscience began to bother him, you know you are wrong, you need to be on the inside instead of the outside, but he kept on until almost the 11'o clock hour and the strange feeling kept nudging and pulling on him. He kept riding until he

could almost not hear the church bell ringing. He says to his horse woe, saying to himself I'm almost out of hearing distance of the church bell. He says to his peer group I don't have time to explain, but I see you yawl later. He then turns his horse around and started to make his way back to the church house. The moral of the story is that there can be people inside the church and is not within hearing distance.

28. If you want your prayers heard. Psalm 1:2: But his delight is in the law of the Lord and in his law he meditates day and night. You can learn how to follow God by meditating on God's Word. This means spending time reading and thinking about what you have read.

29. It means asking yourself how you should change so you're living, as God wants. Knowing and thinking about God's Word are the first steps toward applying it to your everyday life. If you want to follow God more closely, you must know what he says.

30. If you want success remember Joshua 1:8: This book of the law shall not depart out of thy mouth; but thou shalt meditate therein day and night, that thou may observe to do according to all that is written therein: for THEN thou shalt make thy way prosperous, and THEN thou shalt have good success.

31. Psalms 1:3: He shall be like a tree planted by the rivers of waters that bring forth its fruit in its season. Whose leaf shall not wither, and whatsoever he does

shall prosper. I must not turn away my ear from hearing the law, the Word of God.

32. To achieve anything worthwhile, our prayers must not be an abomination to God. We need to be like Jesus, though He wrestles with the flesh as in His temptation, but He could say and thou Father has heard Me and will always hear Me.

33. Well one Friday they crucified Him out on a hill called Calvary. He died when He got ready, no man took His life He laid it down, and they took Him and laid Him in Joseph's new tomb. He stayed there three days and three nights, but early that Sunday morning He rose and step out on resurrection ground and declared that all power in heaven and earth is in my hand. He ascended back to the Father and presented Himself to the Father Holy on our behalf. He return to earth showed Himself to His disciples and hung around for 40 days, being seen by 5000 all at once. Then He boarded a cloud and went back up to heaven while the people stood gazing, and the angels said to them why stand here gazing for the same way you see Him going he is coming back again.

BARRIERS TO ANSWERED PRAYER SERMON #5

SCRIPTURE REFERENCE James 4:1- 4
DELIVERED November 20, 2016
INTRODUCTION

My brothers and sisters, perhaps it has come as a shock to you that there is anything that will bar our prayers from being heard since and I quote "Our God is a Prayer hearing God", but there are many things that will bar our prayers that God's children are ignorant off though they are in His word.

2. Listen one does not look for something that they feel does not exist; and God not hearing you when we pray is a No, No, we have made it not be a part of His nature. We tell ourselves that we can release the power of God through prayer into our situation at will.

3. When God is silent. Are you tempted to think that He doesn't care about the situation you are in or worse

yet he doesn't care about you? Do you find yourself becoming discouraged when you pray to God, asking for something and nothing happens?

4. There are many barriers in the Bible that we erect and we have been shown four. We looked last Sunday at the barrier that was found in Proverb 28:9 which said one who turns away his ear from hearing the law, even his prayers is an abomination. Meaning your prayers nauseate Him, make Him sick, they are disgusting to Him.

5. FIRST we have "**The Revelation.**" The Lord revealed something to us this past Wednesday night during Bible study. It was a profound revelation as it relates to Him and the power of prayer. It came from a discussion I had with a child of God about the barriers God has been giving us in prayer.

6. I told the one to whom I was sharing that God wasn't going to leave us there, that He was going to give us what it takes to get a prayer through. The child of God's response was I'm going to be eavesdropping then.

7. That brought about the revelation from God, that it takes both to release His power through prayer. It takes knowing what the barriers are along with knowing what to do to have success in answered prayer. The Spirit of the Lord illustrated it through a car battery. One has to have both the negative and the positive connected. To release the power from within

the battery.

8. Listen: One connected without the other will produce no power. The congregation was told that the negatives post were the four barriers that Lord has already given us that will bar our prayers from being heard. Don't forget them, because they were going to need them.

9. WHY? Because once you receive what it takes to get a prayer through which can be labeled as a positive post? Listen: A battery fully charged has the have the negative and the positive connected together for power to flow. Therefore we need to eavesdrop now as well as then as He gives us one more negative before He starts giving us the positives, we all need Him to release His power in answers to our prayers.

10. SECONDLY we have "**The Fifth Barrier.**" It is found in James chapter 4 which is "Praying Amiss", that is praying with the wrong motives. Desiring things that are not for the glory of God, and the good of others, but only to spend it upon your own intemperate lusts and pleasures.

11. Verse 1 of the text lets us know that war and fighting come among us from our desires for pleasure that war in our members. Conflicts and disputes among believers are always harmful. James lets us know that these quarrels result from evil desires battling within us. We want more possessions, more money, higher status, and recognition. When we don't get what we

want, we fight in order to have it.

12. James tells us that it is not enough to ask for good things, but we must ask with a good spirit and intention. He says "Ye ask amiss, that ye may consume it upon your lusts, literally your pleasures and not that ye may have the things you need for the service of God.

13. Praying amiss is praying for the things of this life only that you may please the flesh, and gratify your carnal appetites. You do it with a view to self-indulgence and carnal gratification. Therefore while we would have God serve our lusts we bar our prayers. The text says ye receive not because you ask amiss, ye ask to consume it upon your lust.

14. In prayer we must consider three things, the object, the manner, and the end: We must not only guard our affections, but secure our intentions; our motives, for prayers that choose a good aim, do also highlight a good issue; ye ask, and receive not because ye ask amiss.

15. Instead of having an attitude about what we want, we should submit ourselves to God, ask God to help us get rid of our selfish desires, and trust Him to give us what we really need. God is concerned about your inside, your heart, and not just your outside.

16. Now there is something that James tells us that is one of the most common problems in prayer: not asking at all, asking for the wrong things, or asking for

the wrong reasons. We should think more of God and things pertaining to Him than things pertaining to us.

17. Our prayers will become powerful when we allow God to change our desires so that they perfectly correspond to his will for us. Then you will receive if you obey and do what pleases him because you will be asking in line with God's will. 1 John 5:14: If we ask anything according to His will, He hears us and if we know He hears us, we have the petition we desire of Him.

18. THIRDLY we have "The Present World" In verse 4 of our text James says: You adulterers and adulteress, don't you realize that friendship with this world makes you an enemy of God? I say it again, that if your aim is to enjoy this world, you can't be a friend of God.

19. Selfish desires, according to James lead to war. This spirit of strife is worldliness; it is not Christian, and it is not the Christian approach. These are the things that represent the old nature. A man must be regenerated by faith in Christ and be indwelt by the Holy Spirit.

20. What James describes here is the spirit of the world. When the spirit of the world gets into the church, you have a worldly church. My Bro. and Sis, do you think it is bad out on the battlefield? Do you think it was bad in the Iraq war? Well, it was, but inside some churches and inside the hearts of some individuals it is just as bad.

21. In the business and political world there is dog-eat-dog competition – that's worldliness. Political parties split, and one group becomes pitted against another. One president after being elected to office destroys the work of his predecessor.

22. Listen: As capital and labor meet around the conference table, there is a battle going on. In the social world, there are climbers on the social ladder who are stepping on the hands of others as they go up. That worldliness.

23. In your neighborhood and mine one family does not speak to another family. Within families, there are quarrels, brother against brother, sisters against sisters. Then that spirit gets into the church. That, my brothers and sisters, is worldliness. Yet ye have not because ye ask not.

24. Our desires should be taken to the Lord in prayer, to have them satisfied or denied or refined, and then we need to accept the answer from Him. What is the cure for worldliness? It is prayer. It is faith in God. The apostle John put it like this, "For whatsoever is born of God overcometh the world."

25. He says and this is the victory that overcometh the world, even our faith. The answer is to trust in God absolutely, to go to Him in prayer, and commit to Him that which is in your heart. When you find that there is strife and envy in your heart, talk to God about it.

26. One theologian says: Many of us go to the Lord to tell Him how good we are. And because we have been good little boys and girls who have gone to Sunday school, we think He ought to give us a lollipop or a Brownie button or some other kind of reward.

27. FOURTHLY and I bid you good morning, we have "The Cure" There is a cure for worldliness. Tell God all that is in your heart, as one unloads one's heart, its pleasures, and its pains, to a dear friend. Tell Him your troubles, that He may comfort you; tell Him your joys, that He may sober them.

28. Tell Him your longings, that He may purify them; tell Him your dislikes, that He may help you to conquer them. Talk to Him of your temptations, that He may shield you from them; show Him the wounds of your heart, that He may heal them.

29. Lay before Him all your indifference to good, your depraved tastes for evil, and your instability. Tell Him how self-love makes you unjust to others, how vanity tempts you to be insincere, how pride disguises you to yourself and to others. You don't need to go to a psychiatrist and lay on his couch, you need to go to God and lie on His couch and pour your heart out to Him. That is what the Psalmist David did in Psalms 51 and that is what I have had to do.

30. If you pour out all your weaknesses, needs, and troubles, there will be no lack of what to say. You will never exhaust the subject. It is continually being

renewed. People who have no secrets from each other are never without a subject of conversation.

31. They do not weigh their words, for there is nothing to be held back. Neither do they seek for something to say. They talk out of the abundance of the heart, without consideration, just what they think. Blessed are they who attain such familiar, unreserved intercourse with God.

32. Another theologian asks the question: Are we trying to kid ourselves that we are nice, sweet, little folk who have no envy and jealousy in our hearts? I heard a woman say one time, "I have a very wonderful husband. He is not jealous of me.

33. I want you to know that something is wrong with that picture. If a husband is not jealous of his wife, you can question his love. If he loves her, he will be jealous of her. God loved the children of Israel and He told them that He is a jealous God.

34. But know my brothers and sisters that there can be jealousy in the wrong sense like jealousy when you do not receive recognition in the church that you feel we deserve. And what about the strife we cause with our tongues?

35. I came to the conclusion that I was going to tell the Lord Jesus everything. We all need to talk to Him about everything in our lives that was sinful and questionable. He knows, He understands, I have done

it and He's forgiven me.

36. Listen: I reiterate, to be healed of praying amiss, you don't need to go to the psychiatrist; he'll just move your problem from one area to another. You need to get rid of that hang-up by going to the Lord Jesus, getting on His couch, and telling Him everything.

37. We can do this because one Friday they hung Him high and straight Him wide out on a hill called Calvary. He died when He got ready, no man took His life He laid it down, and they took Him and laid Him in Joseph's new tomb. He stayed there three days and three nights, but early that Sunday morning He rose and step out on resurrection ground and declared that all power in heaven and earth is in my hand. He ascended back to the Father and presented Himself to the Father Holy on our behalf. He return to earth showed Himself to His disciples and hung around for 40 days, being seen by 5000 all at once. Then He boarded a cloud and went back up to heaven while the people stood gazing, and the angels said to them why stand here gazing for the same way you see Him going he is coming back again.

SUCCESS TO ANSWERED PRAYER SERMON #1

SCRIPTURE REFERENCE Proverbs 15:8-9
DELIVERED November 27, 2016
INTRODUCTION

My brothers and my sisters, the Bible is saturated with things that are "Barriers to Answered Prayer." He has lifted up and expounded on five of them. He has made it clear that they are not to be forgotten, but remembered.

2. He illustrated the release of His power in answer to prayer, through the way you get power out of a car battery. The barriers serve as the negative post that must be connected with the positive post to release the power from within.

3. Isn't God good, or can say it this way ain't God good. Don't you just love Him. He starts today giving us some positives. This is just one of many within the

Bible. Note the latter part of Proverbs 15:8: But the prayer of the upright is his delight.

4. Listen: God has such a love for the upright that their prayer is a delight to him. Praying graces are the work of His own Spirit in the upright, with which He is well pleased to hear and answer their cry unto Him in prayer.

5. Though our approach to God is not at the expense of an ultimate sacrifice [He Himself has provided that]. The upright, God not only answers their prayers, but He delights in hearing their voices in prayer, and in doing them good.

6. The prayer of the upright is His delight. What a motive to be upright in lifestyle; and what a motive it is to the upright in prayer! But who are the upright? He or she are the ones who are weary of sin, and sincerely desires the salvation of God.

7. The upright are those who have already received a measure of that salvation. Therefore it is said in the next verse, "He loves him that follows after righteousness." He loves he who earnestly desires, and diligently endeavors to be holy and righteous in the course of his or her life.

8. FIRST we have "**What Prayer Reveals.**" Prayer is one of the surest tests both of Christian conviction and Christian character. The clear consciousness and firm conviction of God compel frequency and gladness in

prayer, for not only does God delight in it, you do too.

9. Prayer is often hard and exhausting work. It is often difficult, because our hearts are idle and wayward; and because prayer is essentially the submission of our will, and of all the hard things to do, none is harder than the surrender of the will.

10. There is peace and strength in prayer, but there is also toil and unspeakable sacrifice. God protects us, in our prayers, against ourselves. He will not suffer our ignorance to be our ruin, He only grants such prayers as are for our own good.

11. The character of a Christian can be almost unmistakably told by the nature of his prayer. Prayer is a crucial standard of one's spiritual life. If you want to know about a child of God, just listen to him or her pray. What is this prayer? Words are generally, not always, necessary to pray. There are occasions when prayers in words are impossible.

12. SECONDLY we have "**What Prayer Renders.**" God's delight in the prayer of the upright: God takes great pleasure in the prayers of upright men, women, boys and girls. He even calls them HIS delight. Therefore our first concern is to be upright.

13. Upright: What is it? It bending neither this way nor that, not crooked with policy, nor powerless by yielding to evil. Be ye upright in strict integrity and straight-forwardness. If we begin to shuffle and shift

to make it in any endeavor, we shall be left to shift for ourselves.

14. If we try crooked ways to attain, we shall find that we cannot pray right, and if we pretend to do so, we shall find our prayers shut out of heaven. Are you acting in a straight line, and therefore following out the Lord's revealed will? Then let us pray much, and pray in faith.

15. If our prayer is God's delight, then let us not rob Him in that which gives Him pleasure. He does not consider the grammar, the technical precepts and practical arts of our prayer, nor the words of it; in all these men might despise how one pray to God.

16. God as a Father takes pleasure in the lisping of His own babes, the stammering of His newborn sons and daughters. Should we not delight in prayer since the Lord delights in it? Let us make hast to the throne. The Lord gives us more than enough reasons for prayer, and we ought to be thankful.

17. THIRDLY we have "**What Prayer Represents.**" I think the prayer of the upright is here put in distinction and in contrast to the sacrifice of the wicked. The wicked man may go to great pains to provide something more than a prayer.

18. It may even cost him something considerable. He may wear himself out in labor for Christ and His church, but he has not attended to the main matter;

his heart goes not with the sacrifice. Then on the other hand, here is an upright man, who, perhaps, has no opportunity for offering special gifts.

19. He comes with groaning and before it reaches heaven it is transformed into a song. Now, why does the Lord take such pleasure in the mere prayer of the upright? Because it is a sign of life and not just living. It may be feeble, but it is an indication that there is life to the distressed one.

20. The prayer of the upright is God's delight, for He says within Himself, "My child still lives; his spiritual pulse is beating, his lungs are working, for his prayer ascends into My holy temple like a sweet smelling aroma in My nostril.

21. The prayer of the upright is an indication of health. One is not content with just merely being alive: but you want to be lively as well as living; let me tell you, you want to be all the way alive? Therefore is the prayer of the upright God's delight.

22. God sees that His little ones are buoyant, hearty, and wholesome. This is to Him as the sparkling eye and the rosy cheek of health, and He is glad within Himself when He sees His offspring's rejoicing in fullness of vigor in their prayer life, praying with faith and confidence.

23. Their prayers are proof of confidence. We all like to be trusted. Again, prayer is a token of gratitude. One

can almost hear God saying, this needy child of God is glad of the blessing that I gave him yesterday, for he is at My feet again today asking for more.

24. He appreciates My delivering power in the past, for he is calling for more mercy still. I will be encouraged to bless him. God is glad to treat all believing hearts this way. God will delight in the prayers of the upright because He sees how beneficial it is for us to pray.

25. Listen: Apart from the joy that He Himself receives, He is well aware that it brings joy to our hearts. I don't want you to suppose where I'm with prayer. So let me tell you. I believe that prayer moves the arm of God.

26. I am persuaded that it touches His heart, stirs Him to action, and causes Him to stretch forth His saving hand. Let me add to the fact that prayer is a relief to my own mind, and the fact that it gives God pleasure to hear me pray, causes me to make prayer a way of life.

27. This my brother and sisters is what keep me, and I can say now that that is what keep me praying, if I had no other assurance. The prayer of the upright being His delight. That alone is a stimulus to constant intercession.

28. FOURTHLY and I bid you good morning, we have "**What Prayer Releases.**" There is something about the prayer of the upright that-particularly rejoices God's heart. The upright prayers are humble prayers. They

are as the snowdrops of the spring-time, or as the violet of the early summer.

29. There is something about it so pleasing, that God looks on it with great delight. It does not hold up its head like the glaring sunflower that seems to invite attention. It is like the prayer of the Publican rather than that of the self-admiring Pharisee.

30. The prayer of the upright is earnest. They are pointed; they do not deal with generalities, but with details. They are marked "Urgent". Especially is it the faith of the prayer that pleases God. Faith brings the promises in the form of a check for God to cash.

31. The prayer of faith seems to say: "Lord", do as Thou hast said; remember Thy word to Thy servant, upon which Thou hast caused him to hope. The prayers that God delights in are full of the spirit of resignation, faith and submission. They should go hand in hand.

32. And know this brothers and sisters God the Father rejoices when He sees the name of Jesus upon the prayer. How gladly does He recognize the aroma of Christ's merit and the fragrance of His death! Prayers presented by you in Jesus' name and then presented by Jesus Christ in your name must give our God great joy.

33. Listen: For even with Him it is more blessed to give than it is to receive. He delights in your prayer even when He keeps you waiting, for He will send the answer just when you most need it. When He waits He

knows it wouldn't be well for you to have your answer earlier.

34. Well one Friday they crucified Him out on a hill called Calvary. He died when He got ready, no man took His life He laid it down, and they took Him and laid Him in Joseph new tomb. He stayed there three day and three nights, but early that Sunday morning He rose and step out on resurrection ground and declared that all power in heaven and earth is in my hand. He ascended back to the Father and presented Himself to the father Holy on our behalf. He return to earth showed Himself to His disciples and hung around for 40 days, being seen by 5000 all at once. Then He boarded a cloud and went back up to heaven while the people stood gazing, and the angels said to them why stand here gazing for the same way you see Him going he is coming back again

SUCCESS TO ANSWERED PRAYER SERMON #2

SCRIPTURE REFERENCE 2 Kings 20:1-6
DELIVERED December 4, 2016
INTRODUCTION

My brothers and my sisters, the Lord is instructing us as He did the twelve. He is teaching us by way of a parable to illustrate how we are to get power out of Him in answer to our prayers. Parable teaching is using an earthly means, something that everybody is familiar with to make a spiritual point.

2. He used the power source of an automobile, which is the battery that must have a negative and positive post connected to the battery. He gave us last Sunday one of many positives post, for the Bible is filled with them also. One of which is what stated in the latter part of Proverbs 15:8: But the prayer of the upright is His delight.

3. Today He gives us another from the way Hezekiah prayed: FIRST we have "**The Plea in His Prayer.**" Note verse 3: "I beseech thee, O Lord, remember now how I have walked before thee in truth and with a perfect heart, and have done that which is good in thy sight.

4. Hezekiah was a normal person just like you and I. He was wondering why he was being cut off in the midst of his days at the age of thirty-nine, when wicked kings as Uzziah live to be [68] and Rehoboam who live to be [58] and they did what was evil in the Lord sight.

5. Hezekiah's plea that he had lived a good life was an argument that succeeded with God. It is worthy for us to observe that the prayers recorded in the Old Testament are full of argument. Men approach God with reasons. They could tell Him why He should grant their requests.

6. Now on the surface Hezekiah plea looks like a self-righteous plea. But there is no Pharisaical self-righteousness with him. He is only conscious of the fact that he has honestly en-deavored to serve God, and to do his will.

7. Hezekiah pleads his uprightness and holy conduct in his own behalf. Was it sinful to do so? No; but one could say he was not showing much humility either, for approached God from the position of having a perfect heart.

8. If he had a perfect heart, who made it such? It was

God. In his doing good in God's sights who enabled him to do so? It was God. Could he therefore plead on his behalf character and actions that he wouldn't have had but by the power of the grace of God?

9. I don't think so. But the times of this ignorance God winked at. The Gospel teaches us a different lesson. Jesus says in: Matthew's 23:12: And whosoever shall exalt himself shall be abased; and he that humbles himself shall be exalted.

10. Does this mean we can't approach God like Hezekiah? NO because we are told in Hebrew's 4:16 Let us therefore come boldly unto the throne of grace that we may obtain mercy, and find grace to help in time of need.

11. There are means [IF] we are being true to God that can be used by us to keep life and health in our lives. We ought to use them with a strong wish to live. This is resignation to God's will. In desiring life, and loving many days that you might see the best things of life.

12. Listen: When you know you have surrendered all and is a beloved disciple, a lover of Jesus Christ and His word, and it can be said of you as He said of Mary; she has chosen the good part, and it shall not be taking away from her. She sat at Jesus feet and heard His word, while....Etc.

13. SECONDLY we have "**The Purpose of His Prayer.**" Hezekiah did not feel that he had been disobedient or

un-sub-missive. Now there are saintly souls living upon the earth today through which the Lord is bestowing blessing in homes, communities, schools, and the work place. A true story is told of an employee that works for this particular company that was a child of God and lived unashamedly as a child of God. When this employee retires they are given high recognition by the other employees. Then it wasn't long before a very unpleasant change came upon that particular work place of the company. After a while the child of God that retired decided to go back to the place to visit because they had a good relationship with the other workers. They were met with the words when you retired things got really gotten bad around here, they were told that when you retired Jesus let the building.

14. Hezekiah recounted mercies past as a reason for expecting renewed favors, and spoke of His goodness; of their great needs for His help. Therefore because of brevity of life he laid claim to mercy. So he did not hesitate to find in his past life reasons for his to continue.

15. Watch This: He desired to live, not so much for his own sake, as for that of his family and people of God. He wanted to live especially for the interests of true religions and he prayed to that effect with many tears as well as with great fervency.

16. His lamentation, from what is known as liquid prayers. On this occasion caused God to hear the voice

of his weeping. The Lord knew, and Hezekiah knew he could appeal to the God that way, that he had walked before Him in sincerity and uprightness of heart.

17. He refuses to believe that goodness makes the term of life shorter, or more uncertain. Hezekiah knew the Word Proverbs 3:2: My son forgets not my law; but let thine heart keep my commandments: For length of days, long life, and peace, shall they add to thee.

18. He was not conscious that he had omitted anything that was to be done for the restoring of the true worship of God, in which he had been so faithful in laboring to take away the high places of idol worship that had continued ever since the time of David.

19. When Hezekiah saw the nation in danger of false religion because of the invasion of the Assyrian army. They threatened to destroy the religion of the true God. He was greatly affected at the news of his death, therefore he wept sorely.

20. THIRDLY and I bid you good morning, we have "The Principle of the Prayer" The nation at that time was endangered with an assault by the whole force of the king of Assyria. No one had removed them; and therefore he presumed to beg that he might live, to settle and establish what he had begun to do.

21. He wished to live to see the enemies of God overthrown. And therefore God promises that He will deliver the city out of the hands of the king of Assyria,

at the same time that He promises him a period of fifteen more years to live.

22. The people therefore needed a commander, who had wisdom, courage, and faith, to lead them in such an emergency. If he was removed in death, and they were left to an opposed government, Jerusalem would share the fate of Samaria.

23. Therefore with great earnestness and perseverance, Hezekiah had brought his reformation to a hopeful establishment; but he feared the instability of the people and the dissensions of the nobles, would subvert all if he were taken away.

24. He as king having used his authority to suppress idolatry and wickedness, and by every means to promote the worship and service of God. He had done what was good and pleasing in God sight, being an example to his people.

25. The consciousness of his integrity gave him confidence; and he begged the Lord to remember the fruits of grace which had been produced, and to spare him, that he might be yet more fruitful and useful. Note where his heart is. His motive for praying is weighted down with God concerns.

26. True religion lengthens men's lives and crowns their hopes. What man is he that loves life? Let him fear God, and that will secure him from many things that would influence his life, and secure to him life

with Christ in this world and in the world to come.

27. The fear of the Lord will add days more than is expected, it will prolong them to the days of eternity. What man is he that would see good days? Let him be true to God, for the hope of the righteous shall be gladness; they shall have what they hope for, to their unspeakable satisfaction.

28. It is God's nature to keep His promises. He loves to hear the loud outcries of needy souls. It is His delight to bestow favors. He is more ready to hear than we are ready to ask. Especially on the principles of Hezekiah, [Lord remember how I have lived]…Etc.

29. The best results of Hezekiah's prayer are not recorded. He walked before the Lord in solemn gladness. In those remaining years God was nearer to him than before. He knew the tenderness of God, who had heard his prayers and had seen his tears.

30. He knew the grace of God, for by His favor he walked in newness of life. He knew the power of God, whose high prerogative it was to turn backward or forward at His will the dial of his life.

31. How great is the power of prayer, which still appeals to the heart of God and persuades Him to make known His way upon earth, His saving power to bestow health among all nations. Hezekiah asks God for a sign that He had answered him.

32. And God gave him a sign. How infinite is the grace

of God, who in time past for this chosen servant turned backward for an hour the shadow of the sun as a sign that He had answered his prayer.

33. Consider who, in these last days, has set for ever in the spiritual heavens, above the horizon and within the field of vision for those who look in faith, we have the blessed Son of Man, Jesus the Christ.

34. Who one Friday they crucified Him out on a hill called Calvary. He died when He got ready, no man took His life He laid it down, and they took Him and laid Him in Joseph new tomb. He stayed there three day and three nights, but early that Sunday morning He rose and step out on resurrection ground and declared that all power in heaven and earth is in my hand. He ascended back to the Father and presented Himself to the father Holy on our behalf. He return to earth showed Himself to His disciples and hung around for 40 days, being seen by 5000 all at once. Then He boarded a cloud and went back up to heaven while the people stood gazing, and the angels said to them why stand here gazing for the same way you see Him going he is coming back again.

SUCCESS TO ANSWERED PRAYER SERMON #3

SCRIPTURE REFERENCE John 4: 46 - 54
DELIVERED December 14, 2016
INTRODUCTION

My brothers and my sisters the Lord is instructing us as to what is required for His power to be released in answer to our prayers. He has, from a parable perspective, taught us using a very familiar object that will only work when it is properly connected, which is the car battery.

2. His power in answer to prayer is released when there are two connections made to Him. One is knowing what we are not to do, and the other is knowing what we are to do. He has already given us some of what we are not to do. He is now giving us what we are to do.

3. Listen: When it comes to prayer He has shown us the kind He likes to hear and answer. Proverb 15:8: The prayer of the upright is His delight. Then from

2 Kings 20:3, we were shown Hezekiah's plea that he had lived a good life, which was an argument that succeeded with God.

4. Today He gives us another positive. It is "Faith" Now this is the one that is most often lifted. "Faith"; we claim to have it when in actuality we don't. Most think it is an automatic bestowal when it is not. Most think they can have faith without acquiring it in God's way. According to Romans 10, saving faith comes by hearing, and trusting faith comes by obedience.

5. FIRST we have "**The Nobleman Faith.**" He was a father that approach God in prayer on behalf of His son. Human sorrow is the birth pang of prayer. The distressed father's sense of utter powerlessness to help his son drove Him to Christ.

6. He was considered a dignitary a man of importance, but it was no security from the assaults of sickness in his family. Note he was the petitioner himself. His tender affection for his son caused him to spare no pain to get help for him.

7. This government official was not only an officer in Herod's service he was a father. He had walked 20 miles to see Jesus and called him Lord putting himself under Jesus even though he had legal authority over Him.

8. SECONDLY we have "**An Urgent Understanding.**" Listen: When it comes to receiving an answer to our

prayers, there are some things we need to know about God because He is subject to respond to you with a rebuke of your approach and we must react properly and not be shaken by the rebuke, but keep asking even though He has responded that way.

9. Let's examine the criticism the father received from Christ upon his request for help. Jesus says to him "Except you see signs and wonders you will not believe". Here is a man coming to God for help already hurting yet Christ gives him a strong rebuke.

10. Listen: For one's prayers to have success with God, we must accept with a good spirit His reproof, His rebuke, for we are never without the need of admonishment. Note what the Lord is doing. Christ shows this father his weakness and sin to prepare him for mercy, and then grant his request.

11. It is said for those whom Christ intends to honor with His favors He first humble with His frowns, and which of us don't deserve His frowns. The father took the rebuke patiently, he did not take it as an insult, and he did not take it for a denial, but continued making his request until he prevailed.

12. The greatest men when they come to God must become beggars. Note the mixture in his faith his prayer was sincere, and he did believe that Christ could heal his son, but there was also a weakness in his faith.

13. THIRDLY we have "The Father's Problem." He

did not think Christ could heal him at a distance therefore he ask him to come to his house to heal him. We are encouraged to pray, but the principle for us to be guided by is that we are not to perceive in our minds where and how we want our prayers answered.

14. Permit me to get a little technical with you, I don't do this often, but it is required for clarity of what Jesus said to the nobleman. The phrase "Except you see signs and wonders you will not believe" is in the [Greek Aorist Subjective mood] Meaning that Jesus knew that there was some doubt and uncertainty and that the uncertainty arose because the action had not yet occurred. Is that not what brings doubt into our situation as well?

15. We need to understand this: Our blessed Lord did what this man requested Him to do, but not in the way in which he wished it to be done. God will respond to faith in Him to all who call upon Him, but not in the way in which we may desire.

16. Listen: It is God who judges the best way of doing us good. The father wished his son to be healed by Jesus going down to Capernaum. He did it without going to Capernaum. Jesus answered his prayer where He was.

17. His presence was not necessary for the child's healing. "Go thy way thy son liveth." Believing the spoken words of Christ the nobleman returned home and was met by his servants with the good news. Listen:

Good news will meet those who believe God's word.

18. FOURTHLY we have "**The Strange Question.**" The father asks what hour his son began to recover. A strange question. Strange because most are not concerned about when or how their prayer is answered, they just want an answer. Something must have happened to this father for him to ask such a question.

19. He must have received some assurance, evidently right after the Lord told him to go thy way thy son liveth, I believe the moment he believed, the Lord gave him an assurance that everything was going to be alright. He does know when one has believed Him.

20. There was a double effect instantaneously: The man believed Jesus' words, and the cure, moved quicker than lightning from Cana to Capernaum and was felt by the dying son. As evidence of full faith, the father leaves Christ and heads for home.

21. The servant was in a hurry to tell the anxious parent the good news. The father wanted to know when it happens, his faith wanted confirmation. When did he begin to amend? Yesterday, at the seventh hour, the fever left him, it was the very hour in which was uttered the great word, "Thy son liveth!

22. He desired to have his faith confirmed because He knew what came over him the same hour the Lord told him to go thy way thy son liveth. The diligent association of the works of Christ with what He has

done for us will strengthen and confirm our faith every time but most of us are not interested in associating the work of Christ with what He has done for us.

23. The healing of this father's son was more than a favor to one official; it is for all the people. John's Gospel was written to all humankind to urge faith in Christ. Here a government official had faith that Jesus could do what He claimed.

24. The father knew that there was power in Jesus' words. This government official not only believed that Jesus could heal; he also demonstrated his faith in Jesus "Go thy way thy son liveth", and he continued on his mission. It is believed that the Father didn't even go home to check.

25. FIFTHLY we have "The Father Action" It isn't enough for us to say we believe that Jesus can answer our prayers. We need to act upon our beliefs. He obeyed when the Lord told him to go thy way, and while he was on his way He received his answer. Do you want to receive an answer? Then obey God when He tells you to do something whether it makes sense or not. Remember the ten lepers who came to Jesus....Etc.

26. Although we are not told what mission the nobleman was on, his son was healed when Jesus spoke the word. Distance is no problem for Christ because He has mastery over space. His power transcends any distance. He can just speak a word and it is done from wherever He is.

27. The faith of parents and their prayers to Jesus Christ are often the means of unspeakable blessings to their children; and however distant they may be from home, their friends or from Christ, His power can reach them, and His grace can supply their wants.

28. Faith is a gift that grows as we use it. He believed and that compelled him to go to Cana to ask for the Lord's help, he believed the words of Christ when he was told to go his way thy son liveth. This is how faith is built up to maturity.

29. Notice how the nobleman's faith grew. First, he acted on it through obedience, a major requirement for prayers to be answered. Secondly, he believed and received Jesus' assurance that his son would live, and be alright.

30. There is a blessed ending to this story. He had before believed the word of Christ, but now he believes in Christ. Christ's aim is always greater than we can imagine. He was out to gain the heart by the granting of temporal blessing. Temporal blessings always pave the way for spiritual blessing.

31. His whole house likewise believed in Christ. What a blessed change came about in that home because of the sickness of a child. This should change our view toward afflictions; we know not what good may come from them if we just turn to God in prayer.

32. All of this can happen for us because one Friday

they hung Him high and straight Him wide out on a hill called Calvary. He died when He got ready, no man took His life He laid it down, and they took Him and laid Him in Joseph's new tomb. He stayed there three days and three nights, but early that Sunday morning He rose and step out on resurrection ground and declared that all power in heaven and earth is in my hand. He ascended back to the Father and presented Himself to the Father Holy on our behalf. He return to earth showed Himself to His disciples and hung around for 40 days, being seen by 5000 all at once. Then He boarded a cloud and went back up to heaven while the people stood gazing, and the angels said to them why stand here gazing for the same way you see Him going he is coming back again.

SUCCESS TO ANSWERED PRAYER SERMON #4

SCRIPTURE REFERENCE 1 Kings 18:30-39
DELIVERED December 21, 2016
INTRODUCTION

My brothers and sisters, true religion has nothing to conceal, nothing to hide. It can invite people to come near to examine closely the facts. Truth begs to be examined, investigated, and scrutinized; for when it is, it will shine forth in its glory to God.

2. Jesus said to search the scriptures, examine them; study them closely; look at them in detail. You will not come away in disbelief. The Bible is not weak in its claims that we dare not search it for fear of being disappointed. You will come away believing and trusting.

3. True religion promotes communion with God. It produces fellowship with God. It does not drive us from God as false religion does. We need this communion

with God. It is absolutely essential to the well-being of our lives.

4. True religion takes us to the Lord who straightens things out in our lives. It knows what the real problem is and what the right answer is to the problem. True religion for us today is the Christian religion; it will put things in order in our lives.

5. FIRST we have "**The Altar.**" The text uniquely opens when it is Elijah's turn to offer sacrifice to God. He calls for the people to come near to him and the people came. He takes 12 stones representing the 12 sons of Jacobs, the 12 tribes of Israel. He repairs the altars of the Lord that were broken down.

6. The great distinctive worship of Jehovah was revealed at the contest on Mount Carmel, it can be seen in the restoration of the altar, the saturation of it with water, the prayer by Elijah to God, and the burning up of the sacrifice and altar by fire from above.

7. The prophet Elijah needed an altar on which to put his sacrifice. So he restored the one on Mount Carmel. I'm going somewhere with this. He restores the altar for a purpose, maybe you need to restore yours, and if there is not one, you need to establish one. A place where you pray unto God?

8. Altars what are they? They can be called devotional time. But whatever we call them, we need to have one in our lives. If your life has been made shambles by the

false religions of the world, come back to the Lord and let Him put your life together again. There is a fairy tale that goes like this: Humpty Dumpty sat on the wall. Humpty Dumpty had a great fall. All the king's horses and all the king's men, couldn't put Humpty Dumpty together again. But the true Christian religion can put your life together again.

9. The altar speaks of communion with God. One's communion with God can be easily discerned by whether or not he or she has an altar in their life. As an example, when Abraham was in good communion with God, he had an altar. But when he went astray, he left the altar.

10. SECONDLY we have "**The Sacrifice on the Altar.**" Listen: Two items especially attract our attention on the altar of Elijah day. One was the sacrifice, which was a bullock. A bullock was a sin offering. It recognized the sinfulness of man and the need for the mercy of God. How appropriate this was in the case of Israel.

11. Sin was the problem in the land of Israel, Sin brings disorder and confusion. God's mercy was desperately needed to forgive the people and heal the land. Elijah laid the wood upon the altar in order, and then a bullock was laid upon the Altar.

12. Elijah put the wood in order; this tells us that he would do things decently and in order in the Lord's work. God's work demands we do things right. It is a spirit of ungratefulness to the Lord to see how

disorganized things get when it comes to giving Him what He will respond to.

13. Listen: After putting the wood in order and cutting the bullock in pieces he had them to fill four barrels with water, and pour it on the burnt sacrifice and on the wood. After this was done, he had it repeated two more times, saturating them with water.

14. False prophets could not get a fire started in the middle of the day when the sun was the hottest and when everything was kindling dry. But true prophets can start a fire when the sacrifice, wood, etc. are thoroughly saturated with water.

15. The water demonstrated the power of God, and the priority of the Word. The power of God in working on our behalf in our daily lives. God delights to work when conditions are the worst, and He often lets our circumstances get drenched with impossibilities before He works. This is a principle for us to remember.

16. He does this to assure that He will be given the glory. So it was on Mount Carmel. It was obvious in this contest that the circumstances were being arranged so Baal would have every advantage compared to Jehovah.

17. The second thing the water demonstrated was the priority of the Word. Elijah poured water on the altar because God commanded it. It did not look like the smart thing to do; in fact, it looked like it would hinder

the desired result. But Elijah obeyed, for true believers put great priority on the Word.

18. Are you willing to put the Word in such a prominent place in your life? Will you obey the Word of God even though its commands look impractical and impossible? Are we willing to obey the Word even though it seems to oppose what we are doing rather than support it?

19. THIRDLY we have "**The Prayers on the Altar**" Elijah, as did the prophets of Baal, prayed before the altar. But Elijah praying was not like the praying of the prophets of Baal. It did not include loud shouting, and it was not accompanied by cutting themselves like Baal prophets.

20. Watch This: The dignity of Elijah's prayer is seen in the four requests he made to God. # 1. He prayed for the glory of God: Let it be known this day that thou art God in Israel. It was not rain first, but God's glory first. The reason for their problems was that God was not first.

21. In our praying we must correct the lack of honor for God. Our prayers need to be about God first and our need second. True Christian disciples make their primary petition and desires of their prayers to be the glory of God. There are far too many who claim to love God does not do this.

22. Number # 2. He prayed for his own testimony. He said; Let it be known this day that I am thy servant.

This was not bragging. This was a wise prayer that says he wants everyone to know for whom he lives and for whom he serves.

23. Now: That is not an easy prayer to pray when you are outnumbered 450 to 1 as Elijah was. It is not an easy prayer to pray when the crowd is not on your side. Too often in such situations, folk hope no one will find out that they confess to being a Child of God.

24. But Elijah wanted the world to know where he stood. True disciples are not ashamed. Are you willing to be this kind of testimony for Christ in the midst of great ungodliness? Are you willing to pray that others know where you stand regarding Jesus Christ? Your answer will reveal the genuineness of your faith.

25. Number # 3: Elijah prayed for the exalting of God's Word. He said; Let it be known this day that I have done all these things at thy word. As was noted earlier, true disciples will put great emphasis on the Word of God. They will desire the Word to be front and center and will want the Word to have authority in their lives.

26. False religion talks more about other books and writings than they do about the Bible. And carnal churches give themselves away by their lack of emphasis on the Word. Many churches which claim to have a solid foundation do not give much place to the Word in their ministries.

27. Such churches, though they have a fundamental

name and reputation, are not good churches. Get into a church that gives much attention to the Word of God. Remember where the Word is not emphasized, you have evidence of spiritual corruption. You should avoid that at all costs.

28. Number #4: Elijah prayed for revival among the people. He said, Hear me, O Lord hear me, that this people may know that thou art the Lord God, and that thou hast turned their heart back again. Note: He still has not prayed for rain yet!

29. He was wise; they needed revival before they needed rain. Mankind's primary need is spiritual, not material; and true Christian religion puts the emphasis on people's on their spiritual needs and not on social programs. Keep first things first. It is revival then rain, and not rain then revival.

30. Listen: If it was proven that Jehovah God was greater than Baal before the revival they would have missed it if he hadn't had the revival first. That which reveals much decay in churches today is an increased emphasis on social, physical, and material needs over spiritual needs.

31. Recreation is getting more attention than consecration. More emphasis is being placed on suppers than sermons. We have fewer Bible classes and preaching times at our churches so we can have more time for socializing and watching major sports games. Any time you will show a professional football game

on the church monitors right after worship says that the pleasure of the world is your God. I saw on CNN news that this was done in Dallas.

32. FOURTHLY and I bid you good morning, we have **"Elijah Answer to His Prayer on the Altar."** He had success to answered prayer. The fire fell and consumed everything. What a great demonstration of the power of God! The evidence was overwhelming.

33. Yet, sadly today, in spite of overwhelming evidence, men still reject the proof for truth and cling stubbornly to the error of their way. Note where the fire fell. It did not fall on the people. The great Gospel message of substitution is seen in where the fire fell.

34. Sin demands judgment, and fire speaks of this judgment. Therefore the sacrifice took the judgment so sinners did not have to suffer for it. Our judgmental fire fell on Christ. Christ is the great substitute for our sins.

35. He died on the cross because the fiery judgment of God fell on Him instead of on us. When Christ said, "I thirst" it was more than just a physical problem, it spoke of the fire of the judgment of God which came upon Him for our sins.

36. The rich man in hell in Luke 16 cried for water because he was experiencing the fiery judgment of God upon him for his sins. Christ was not his Savior; so he suffered for his own sins and is still suffering in the fire.

But we do not have to have the fire fall on us.

37. We can come to Christ and be saved through Him from the just judgment due for our sins. That is the great message of the true Christian religion. It does not focus on works, on our own merits, on our own blood-shedding as of Baal's prophets; but it focuses on Christ's blood on the cross for us.

38. Let me tell you the gospel story: One Friday, they hung Him high, and straight Him wide out on a hill called Calvary. He died when He got ready, no man took His life He laid it down, and they took Him and laid Him in Joseph's new tomb. He stayed there three days and three nights, but early that Sunday morning He rose and step out on resurrection ground and declared that all power in heaven and earth is in my hand. He ascended back to the Father and presented Himself to the Father Holy on our behalf. He return to earth showed Himself to His disciples and hung around for 40 days, being seen by 5000 all at once. Then He boarded a cloud and went back up to heaven while the people stood gazing, and the angels said to them why stand here gazing for the same way you see Him going he is coming back again.

ACKNOWLEDGMENTS

There are those who have sacrificed greatly that this experience on, "I Know You Pray, But What is Prayer?" was written. There is my wife Irene, and the three children born to us, Yolanda, Patrick III, and Detra, who were brought up to experience and have experienced "The Power of Prayer." To them, we express infinite gratitude for their encouragement and adaptability during a period of the sacrifice of my being a husband, father, and pastor all while following God's lead for me to be in the ministry full-time, fully committed to the cause of Christ and His Church. I deeply appreciate my daughter Detra who graciously assisted me in getting this material ready for publication; she spent many hours working in the tedious process of editing this material.

In addition both within and without this experience in prayer, appreciation goes to my earthly father Patrick H. Tisdale Sr., and my mother Ressie Mae Tisdale (Cross). They both taught us to pray and trust in God, especially my mother, for as a child I would walk upon her in the kitchen with tears rolling down her cheeks. I remember asking her, "Mama why you are crying?", and she would just tell me, "It's going to be alright." I didn't understand then, but now I know she was praying in a way that truly gets God's attention. It's called "Liquid Prayers." According to Psalms 6:8, David asks God to hear the voice of his weeping.

Acknowledgment goes to the late Rev. James R. Grimes (Poppa Grimes) who adopted me as his son in the ministry upon the early death of his youngest biological son. He joined my wife and I in holy matrimony in 1972. He was a loyal preacher pastor who was always there for me, giving me my first revivals in 1974 at St John Baptist Church in Savannah, Tennessee, along with my first baptism in the Tennessee River. Poppa Grimes, as he was affectionately known by all of the preachers in Hardeman County, drilled into us all that people would rather see a sermon any day than hear one, which was his way of telling us to live life as well as preach. Those words govern me to this day.

Acknowledgment goes to the late Rev. Leroy Freeman, my professor at American Baptist College. Acknowledgment also goes to my father-in-law Robert Beauregard, who greatly encouraged me in the field of Christian Education. The above names and many others, too numerous to name, are recognized and treasured in my heart; they all are a part of this whole. Special Thanks must be extended to Djuana Jackson Tomlin, a former member of the Rehoboth Baptist Church. While I was serving as her pastor in the 1990s, she challenged me on the subject of prayer, asking me to teach her how to pray. I ignored her for a long time, thinking to myself, "Everybody knows how to pray." I was coming from my shallow understanding of prayer, but she was insistent and vehemently kept asking the question, "When are you going to teach us how to pray?" She was referring to the congregation as well as herself. In response to her continual inquiries, the study of prayer began, which took us through eleven months of teaching prayer on Wednesdays and ten months of preaching on prayer on Sundays. This book is about the many questions that were asked and responded to during the teaching on prayer and reviewing the sermons that were preached the previous Sunday.

ABOUT THE AUTHOR

Patrick H. Tisdale Jr. a graduate of Middleton High in Middleton, Tennessee. He received his calling into the ministry in 1973, he was licensed in 1974. He graduated from The American Baptist College after five (5) years of study in 1980. Upon graduating, he became an instructor in the school for eight (8) years. He was called to his first pastorage at The Reedy Creek Baptist Church in McClemoresville Tennessee in 1977-1980. His second pastorage was The Oak Hill Baptist Church in Bolivar Tennessee from 1980-1988. His third pastorage was The Cumberland Baptist Church in Jackson Tennessee from 1988-1995. His fourth pasturage is The Rehoboth Baptist Church from 1995 to the present. He challenged himself in biblical studies through not purchasing any spiritual literature for Rehoboth the first seven years. He prepared and taught over three hundred biblical topics, one of which bears the content of this book.

Made in the USA
Middletown, DE
21 August 2024